Introduction

Although the U.S. Army has traditionally focused on conventional warfare, it also has a long history of conducting irregular operations of almost every nature and size. From "winning the west" and Civil War Reconstruction to nation building in Cuba and the Philippines and the occupation duties following both World Wars, the scope of these responsibilities has indeed been immense. Most recently, the Vietnam War and the larger Cold War of which it was a part sparked a renewed interest in both counterinsurgency warfare as well as a broad range of "operations other than war" missions. The employment of Army troops domestically in Civil Rights enforcement, riot control, refugee management, and border security only added to the mix. Doctrinal changes seemed to follow one after the other, while in practice each situation appeared to call for unique solutions and an emphasis on flexibility rather than rote tactical formulas. The Army's recent deployments to Somalia, Haiti, and Bosnia-Herzegovina only reinforced such generalizations.

In Bosnia, the Army worked with its European allies to enforce a negotiated settlement among rival ethnic groups following a long and violent civil war. But no sooner had relative peace come to the area in the late 1990s than another conflict arose to the immediate south when ethnic violence spilled over into the nearby Serbian province of Kosovo. By early 1999, more than eight-hundred thousand ethnic Albanians had been driven out of Kosovo by Serbian forces under Slobodan Milosevic, while as many as twelve thousand may have been murdered in a wave of ethnic cleansing that horrified the world.

Working again in concert with European allies, U.S. forces entered Kosovo in June 1999 with the primary objective of bringing peace to that troubled land. The task, code named Operation JOINT GUARDIAN, proved exceedingly difficult. Entrenched ethnic hatred between Albanians and Serbians continued to fuel the conflict, and the general devastation continued for many weeks. Organized as the Kosovo Forces (KFOR), the Allies were finally able to enforce a tentative peace by October of that year. But as of 2007, the current peacekeeping mission has no end in sight, while the path leading to a larger political solution regarding Kosovo's future has been equally elusive.

The Army's mission in Kosovo was significantly different from the warfighting customarily associated with military service, but it was no less important and no less dangerous. The events surrounding Operation JOINT GUARDIAN have been carefully recorded in this short monograph by R. Cody Phillips. While space limitations do not allow the author to cover every significant event, he has showcased a host of episodes that are common to such missions. The result should both inform the educated soldier and stimulate further study of peacekeeping and peace-enforcement operations.

JEFFREY J. CLARKE
Chief of Military History

Operation Joint Guardian

The U.S. Army in Kosovo

Soon after the North Atlantic Treaty Organization (NATO) introduced a security presence into Kosovo in June 1999, a journalist arranged for an interview with a former Kosovo-Serb paramilitary who had been active in the ethnic cleansing that led to NATO's peacekeeping mission in the Serbian province. The Serb insisted on maintaining his anonymity, but he answered the journalist's questions with unqualified candor. As the interview reached its conclusion, the journalist recounted several horrifying episodes that seemed inexplicable. One in particular was especially puzzling. He asked the young man how he could kill a child. With passionless precision, the paramilitary replied, "You just aim your gun a little lower."

About the same time that this interview occurred and in the eastern part of the province, a Serbian husband and wife drove near a Kosovo-Albanian village. A small band of masked men stopped the vehicle and shot the couple at point-blank range—killing both instantly. A U.S. Army patrol, hearing the gunfire, arrived within minutes and observed "a group of Albanian kids, young kids, cheering from a nearby house, giving the V-sign and doing a knife-cut across their throats."

In the months preceding the arrival of NATO peacekeepers in this war-torn Balkan province, Serbian forces expelled hundreds of thousands of ethnic Albanians from Kosovo. Many of their homes were destroyed, and their property looted by Kosovo-Serbs. Thousands of Kosovars were killed, most of them ethnic Albanians. In the months following the arrival of NATO ground forces, many more Kosovars—Albanian, Serbian, and Roma (or Gypsy)—died. This time, thousands of ethnic Serbs fled the province—their homes burned to the ground, or gutted by explosives, and their property looted by their Kosovo-Albanian neighbors and returning refugees. Many ethnic Albanians and Serbians justified their actions based on ancient calls to avenge the historical wrongs of one people against the other, and to settle scores in long-standing blood feuds. Eventually and only through Herculean effort, the NATO forces—organized as the Kosovo Protection Forces (KFOR)—stopped the violence and enforced the peace that had eluded the region for years.

Strategic Setting

Following World War II, the Communist state of Yugoslavia was organized into six republics, with two "autonomous" regions in the northern and southern portions of Serbia—the largest of the six republics. Technically, the only significant difference between an autonomous region and a republic in Yugoslavia was the tacit understanding that a republic could become self-governing and, if it chose to do so, independent.

The region's history is a volatile one, although the four decades after World War II were relatively calm. With the death of the Yugoslav dictator Josef Tito in 1980, however, and the collapse of communism throughout Eastern Europe, nationalist and ethnic majorities were free to assert claims to self-determination and their desire to separate from Yugoslavia. Slovenia declared its independence in 1991. Croatia, Bosnia-Herzegovina, and Macedonia followed suit over the next two years. The Republic of Montenegro remained within Yugoslavia until 2006, when it, too, voted to separate from the larger state. The northern autonomous province of Vojvodina, with its large ethnic-Hungarian population, remained within Serbia. Conditions in the southern province of Kosovo during the 1990s were significantly less stable.

The history of Kosovo is difficult to follow, in part because its borders have shifted over the years and it has always been a subordinate entity of a larger state. Nominally still a part of Serbia, Kosovo has essentially been a United Nations protectorate since 1999. Its recorded history dates as far back as the first century, when the Roman Empire held sway over the region to mine its rich mineral deposits. By the late twentieth century, roughly 80 percent of the population self-identified as Muslims, reflecting centuries of Turkish influence and the region's place in the former Ottoman Empire; 12 percent of the population identified as Orthodox Christians, and 8 percent as Catholics. These religious identities, however, tended to reflect cultural sentiments or heritage, rather than any deep commitments to particular faiths. Socially, the Albanian population was (and continues to be) highly patriarchal, whereas Serbs have tended to embrace more westernized or egalitarian life styles.

Economically, Kosovo was (and remains today) the poorest region of the Balkans. As of 1979, the annual, per-capita income was $795, barely one-sixth the income obtained in other parts of Yugoslavia. Massive unemployment resulting from the ethnic cleansing and civil turmoil of the 1990s kept the province impoverished well into the next decade. By the late twentieth century, the population was shifting: Serbs, always a minority in Kosovo, were leaving, in part because of increasing tension in the region, but also in order to seek better economic opportunities elsewhere. Hyperinflation, constricting commerce, and limited employment exacerbated discontent among both Albanians and Serbians.

Near the center of the province is the site of the climactic fourteenth-century Battle of Kosovo in which a largely Serbian army fought the invading Ottoman Turks in 1389. The battle was inconclusive, but the Serbs withdrew from the field and, ultimately, the Turks prevailed in the region. In the centuries that followed, the battle achieved near-legendary status, and the site became a historical shrine for Serbians. During this same time frame, populations shifted, with ethnic Serbs concentrating in the central and northern Balkans and ethnic Albanians in the south. More recently, thousands of ethnic Serbs relocated to Kosovo in the early 1990s as a result of civil strife elsewhere in the former Republic of Yugoslavia.

Albanians, who dominated demographically and politically in the southern Balkans for almost five hundred years, usually served the Ottomans, bitter foes of Serbia. Not until the 1870s, when Serbia achieved its independence from the Ottoman Empire, did it become politically feasible for Serbs and Albanians to express their hostility in nationalist-ethnic clashes. Yet beneath the surface stability lay a repressed anger and desire for revenge that was based on each group's differing interpretations of the past.

Between the 1930s and the 1980s, the region once again experienced an ethnic unity artificially enforced by a greater state—Yugoslavia—which muted the conflict between Serbs and Albanians, even after strongman Tito's death, at least for a time.

In 1989, everything changed. Serbian leader Slobodan Milosevic paid an official state visit to Kosovo to mark the anniversary of the famous fourteenth-century battle there against the Turks. He seized the opportunity to solidify his power and authority by invoking nationalist symbols and promising to restore Serbian control over the autonomous province. A minor civil disturbance ensued among Kosovo-Albanians, as well as regional strikes, prompting Milosevic to send ten thousand military personnel into the province to restore order. In 1990, Serbia dissolved the Kosovo assembly, and, in the years that followed, dismissed thousands of ethnic Albanians from government and corporate positions. Although they made up the overwhelming majority, ethnic Albanians soon held not a single position of authority in the Kosovar government, schools, or police force. A shadow government of ethnic Albanians emerged in 1992 to represent the self-proclaimed Republic of Kosovo, but Serbian security forces prevented its parliament from meeting.

Balaton
AUSTRIA
HUNGARY
Slovenia
Ljubljana
Zagreb
Croatia
Bosnia–Herzegovina
SARAJEVO
Montenegro
Podgorica
ADRIATIC SEA
ITALY
YUGOSLAVIA
March 1991
Republic Boundary
0
100 Miles
0
100 Kilometers

Map 1

As the Republic of Yugoslavia split into smaller states throughout the early 1990s, signs of its disintegration commanded international attention, especially the bloody warfare that the independence movement generated in Croatia and Bosnia-Herzegovina. Many ethnic Albanians hoped that their own independence would be achieved through a resolution of the 1995 Dayton Accords, which put an end to the fighting in Bosnia and permitted the entry of a NATO-sponsored peace-enforcement operation into that country. They were bitterly disappointed. Thus it was that, in 1996, a small splinter group of ethnic Albanians resolved to pursue more aggressive means of achieving independence, forming what came to be known in the West as the Kosovo Liberation Army (KLA). (The Kosovo-Albanian name for this organization is the *Ushtria Clirimtare E Kosoves*, which is abbreviated UCK.) Later that year, the KLA launched its first attacks against the police forces in Kosovo. Sporadic fighting, student demonstrations, and strikes continued, even as Serbian security forces became more aggressive in response.

At first, public proclamations by Serbia suggested that it was merely responding to the increasing violence in Kosovo. After 1997, however, it was all too apparent that the Serb infusion of military and paramilitary forces into the region and its expulsion of ethnic Albanians were deliberate moves and ones that had been orchestrated. A careful study clearly indicated that the mass killings (defined as the murder of five or more people) reported at different sites, the acts of vandalism and arson, and the mass migrations were not local aberrations, nor did such incidents arise spontaneously. By August 1998, more than fifteen hundred ethnic Albanians had been killed in the escalating conflict, and almost four hundred thousand had been expelled from Kosovo.

Throughout this time, the United Nations (UN) and the European Union (EU) attempted to prevent a repetition of the tragedy that had only recently been halted in neighboring Bosnia-Herzegovina. With thousands of ethnic Albanians streaming across the border to fill refugee camps hastily established in Macedonia and Albania, the North Atlantic Council, which comprised government representatives of NATO, authorized the activation orders for air strikes against Serbia to halt the violence in Kosovo. Given NATO's public resolve to intervene, a U.S. diplomatic mission to Serbia was able to secure a cease-fire and an assurance that Serbian security forces in Kosovo would be reduced in October 1998. This peaceful resolution of the conflict led to an agreement that allowed two thousand observers from the Organization for Security and Cooperation in Europe (OSCE) to monitor conditions in Kosovo. Called the Kosovo Verification Mission (KVM), the group's intent was to deter further ethnic cleansing in Kosovo. Within months, the effort proved a failure.

Even as the OSCE and Serbian government negotiated for a peaceful resolution of the conflict in Kosovo, thousands of NATO peacekeepers already were scattered throughout the former Yugoslavia to prevent the spread of violence to the other independent republics. A large U.S. Army contingent—Task Force EAGLE—stationed in Bosnia-Herzegovina late in 1995 had achieved sufficient success to permit the number of military personnel to be reduced significantly by 1998. At the time, however, it seemed likely that U.S. forces would remain in Bosnia for several more years.

A much smaller Army task force was located at Camp Able Sentry in what was officially called the Former Yugoslav Republic of Macedonia (FYROM). The U.S. camp was only a few miles north of the Macedonian capital. While Task Force EAGLE labored to prevent further fighting among Bosnians and Serbs, the American forces in Macedonia monitored the border that separated that country from Yugoslavia. The two countries disputed their ill-defined border, often arguing over "mere meters." Through aggressive patrolling, Task Force ABLE SENTRY endeavored to prevent the military forces from Macedonia and Serbia from "bumping into" each other and igniting another armed conflict in the Balkans. As events unfolded in Kosovo, the U.S. military presence in Macedonia and Camp Able Sentry would assume greater prominence in bringing peace to the region.

Conditions in Kosovo deteriorated throughout the winter of 1998–99. The KVM could not stop the violence. KLA attacks became bolder and more frequent among Serbian civilians. Kidnapping, torture, and assassination were common occurrences. Defiant of any political compromise or truce, the KLA taunted the Serb security forces to respond more aggressively, and the Serbs responded as expected. The total personnel strength of all Serbian security forces did not decline, in spite of earlier promises in October 1998 to reduce their numbers.

In fact, the Serbs expelled even more ethnic Albanians from Kosovo. Property in predominantly Albanian neighborhoods was systematically destroyed. OSCE observers noted numerous violations of the peace agreement but rarely were able to stop the violence. Often Serbian paramilitary units surreptitiously entered an Albanian village at night and randomly fired weapons into homes, burned selected buildings, and vandalized property. Ethnic Albanians working in their fields or walking on town streets would be beaten or bullied by roving gangs; sometimes the hapless victims would be robbed, and sometimes they simply disappeared. Even when OSCE observers came forward as witnesses to such attacks, Albanians refused to file formal complaints: Doing so often resulted in more intimidation—or death. The Serbian paramilitary units and the uniformed Yugoslavian security forces (comprised almost entirely of Serbians) dominated this phase of the growing conflict.

The trend pointed toward more violence, and, once warmer weather came to the region, the situation was virtually certain to become worse. In late January, NATO threatened to initiate air strikes against Serbia and forcibly insert a peacekeeping contingent into Kosovo to stop the violence. By early February, the international community was able to prevail upon the Serbian government in Belgrade and the shadow government of the Kosovar-Albanians to meet for talks at Rambouillet, a small town outside Paris, France.

Two extended negotiating sessions took place. The first, held from 6 to 23 February 1999, ended with a tentative resolution that might have brought some measure of peace to the province. Initially, the Serbian delegation was supportive of the agreement, because it provided international guarantees that Kosovo would remain within Serbia. The Albanian delegation, which also included representatives from the KLA,

A typical ethnic Albanian home with enclosed garden in Cernica destroyed during the ethnic cleansing in 1998–99. The cross and four Cs on the left represent a standard sign of Serbian nationalism.

failed to reach a consensus. The conference recessed for three weeks, while the respective governments debated the implications of the proposed agreement. On 15 March, the conference resumed in Paris. This time the Albanian delegation signed the peace agreement; the Serbian delegation did not, largely because of objections to the insertion of NATO peacekeeping forces in Kosovo and the required withdrawal of Serbian security forces from the province. The conference ended on 18 March without resolution.

By that time, thousands of ethnic Albanians were fleeing Kosovo and filling temporary refugee camps in neighboring Albania and Macedonia, sapping the resources of both the host governments and the international relief organizations trying to help the refugees. More fugitives trudged over the snow-capped mountains to safety in Montenegro, and some were able to escape to other European countries, Canada, and the United States. Last-minute efforts by a U.S. delegation sent to Belgrade failed to persuade the Serbian government to sign the peace agreement it had declined to sign in Paris. NATO already had agreed to use air strikes to stop the violence in Kosovo, and it now seemed certain that there would be a military intervention to reverse the deteriorating conditions in the province. On 20 March, OSCE observers withdrew from the region. U.S. diplomatic and military personnel on UN or NATO business left Kosovo hours later. Concurrently, Serbian forces launched a major offensive throughout the province, pushing more refugees across the borders, destroying property, and killing or wounding thousands of civilians.

Operation Allied Force

NATO extended its deadline for a diplomatic resolution three times but to no avail. On 24 March 1999, therefore, a series of orchestrated air strikes hit military, communications, and industrial targets throughout Serbia and Kosovo. Code-named Operation Allied Force, nineteen NATO countries—ranging from Turkey to Iceland and Portugal to Denmark—employed Cruise missiles and a variety of aircraft to pummel the Serbian military. Slobodan Milosevic's command bunker in Belgrade was destroyed and the Serbian infrastructure severely damaged. About thirty-eight thousand sorties were flown during the 77-day air campaign. Of these air strikes, U.S. military aircraft flew more than 60 percent.

The bombing was intense and focused, and NATO expected the air campaign to be a brief one. It was a reasonable expectation. In late summer 1995, a less intensive bombing campaign against Serbian targets hastened an end to the armed conflict in neighboring Bosnia, and it lasted only three weeks. But the Serbs doubted NATO's determination to intervene in Kosovo, especially after U.S. political leaders explicitly denied that American ground troops would invade the province. These mixed signals encouraged Milosevic not to yield early. Then, too, Bosnia had not invoked the same measure of emotional and political attachment that Kosovo did, as Serbians harkened back to its legendary historical significance. Moreover, the mineral wealth of the northern portion of the province still provided some economic benefit. Thus Serbian resolve, as well as posturing, in the face of repeated bombing raids forced NATO to reevaluate its campaign plan.

In the meantime, atrocities multiplied, and hundreds of thousands more ethnic Albanians fled Kosovo in the weeks that followed. This new and sudden surge of refugees into Albania and Macedonia severely strained the resources of international relief organizations. Equally troubling was the possible destabilizing influence that these refugees might pose to the fragile political structures and economies of the host countries. Albania already was the poorest nation in Europe. In spite of its cultural and ethnic sympathy for the refugees, it could do virtually nothing for the Kosovars. Its border along Kosovo was porous, and it was generally accepted that Serbian security forces were indifferent to any violations of Albanian sovereignty. Conversely, Macedonia was inclined to be sympathetic to Serbia and fellow Slavs. (When the air war began, pro-Serb Macedonians rioted and sacked the U.S. embassy in Skopje.) The country already had a large population of ethnic Albanians of its own, and the addition of thousands more was scarcely welcomed by either the Macedonian people or their government. If ethnic Albanians in Kosovo were successful in separating from Serbia, the ethnic Albanian population in Macedonia might try the same thing. This fear was not groundless: Two years later, a small insurgency among ethnic Albanians began in remote northern and western portions of Macedonia.

Early in the air campaign, the U.S. Air Force lost an F–117 "Stealth" aircraft to antiaircraft fire over Belgrade, but the pilot was rescued. More troubling was the capture of three U.S. soldiers from the 1st Squadron, 4th Cavalry, of the 1st Infantry Division at Camp Able Sentry, who were seized by Serbian security forces along the Macedonian-Kosovo border. The three soldiers had been followed for some time before being captured as soon as they strayed into Serbian territory. They were sent to Belgrade and detained for several days before being released. The southern Balkans were tense, and conditions augured worse unless the ethnic cleansing was stopped and the fighting between Serbian forces and the KLA ceased.

Task Force Hawk

As the air campaign continued without any clear end in sight, the number of military targets diminished—in part because the Yugoslav Army dispersed its mobile weapons and equipment and placed the materiel in close proximity to civilian areas. Anticipating this possibility, the NATO command had initiated planning at the start of the air campaign for the deployment of forty-eight AH–64 attack helicopters. These lethal Army aircraft could engage specific targets at close range and minimize the possibility of collateral damage to civilians and nonmilitary facilities. The strike force, soon named Task Force Hawk, was to be positioned in Macedonia, where modest U.S. military support facilities already functioned at Camp Able Sentry. However, on 29 March, the Macedonian government refused NATO permission to launch offensive operations from its soil.

The aviation assets and supporting units for Task Force Hawk would come from U.S. Army Europe (USAREUR), but an operations plan was not published until 22 April. The initial warning order for such a task force, however, came only hours before the bombing campaign began in March. Planning shifted to the alternate site for the base of operations: Albania. The unexpected shift in operational environments was only the beginning of the task force's problems.

The NATO command, anxious to conclude the air war and end the ethnic cleansing that afflicted Kosovo, wanted the task force in place and operational by early April. That deadline was almost certain not to be reached. While planners scrambled to cobble together the requisite organizations and equipment to make Task Force HAWK operational, they also had to arrange for the means of deployment and the support facilities that would be needed in the host country. Even getting some support materials into Albania caused some difficulty—and required imaginative solutions. Some medical supplies were sent using a commercial overnight express company. U.S. Congressional restrictions limited the total force structure that could be deployed to Albania, and the Army leadership expressed some discomfort about using attack helicopters without support from offensive ground forces.

The greatest obstacle was Albania itself. There were no adequate facilities north of the country's national airport outside the capital of Tirana. And even the airport would be vulnerable, if Serbia decided to launch its own attack against NATO forces. Marginal weather, rugged terrain, and a spartan infrastructure to sustain a U.S. base for offensive operations handicapped the task force from the start.

The AH–64 Apaches were drawn from the 11th Aviation Brigade, and the supporting Army aircraft—UH–60 and CH–47 helicopters—came from the 12th Aviation Brigade. Additional aircraft also came from the 30th Medical Brigade. A multiple-launch rocket system (MLRS) and supporting artillery were supplied by USAREUR's V Corps Artillery. The 2d Battalion of the 505th Airborne Infantry from Fort Bragg, North Carolina, and various units from the 2d Brigade of the 1st Armored Division provided ground security. Components of the 7th Support Group rounded out the support package for Task Force HAWK. Lt. Gen. John Hendrix, the commanding general of the U.S. Army's V Corps in Germany, served as the task force commander, with Brig. Gen. Richard Cody and Col. Raymond Odierno assisting as deputy commanders for aviation operations and fire support and ground operations, respectively.

The lead elements for the task force arrived at Rinas Airfield, outside Tirana, Albania, on 9 April. By 26 April, sufficient forces had arrived at the site to declare the task force as mission ready and operational. The final elements arrived on 7 May. Although the task force was never directly employed in Operation ALLIED FORCE, two AH–64 helicopters were lost in Albania, and the pilots died as a result of accidents.

Outside the defense establishment, critics slashed the Army for its apparent timidity or absence of energy in committing assets to the air campaign against Serbia. Political uncertainties, the rapidly assembled and deployed forces, and the extremely austere base of operations in Albania exacerbated the task force's preparations for employment in the air campaign. More troubling was the certainty of losses if helicopters were committed across the border, especially if used without ground support. The Yugoslav Army was known to have an extensive array of air defense weaponry available to combat low-level aircraft. The commitment of Task Force HAWK would significantly alter ALLIED FORCE, reflecting a more intensive war in Kosovo and an increase in casualties on both sides of the conflict. This scenario was not a welcomed one, either by the Army or NATO.

In spite of the awkward commitment of the task force and its conditional value in the air campaign, the consensus among many military observers was that the deployment and presence of Task Force HAWK only one hundred miles from Kosovo engendered some success. The growing U.S. Army presence in Albania attracted the attention of Serbian security forces, which either anticipated the employment of the potent power of the Apache helicopters or feared the continued buildup of an American base of operations that might have led to a ground assault into Kosovo. Notwithstanding this strategic impact on the larger air campaign, Task Force HAWK also demonstrated the Army's ability to create a fighting force to meet a sudden contingency, deploy it to a difficult environment, and make it reasonably operational within only a few days of arrival. Task Force HAWK was not an unqualified success, but its presence in Albania contributed to the eventual conclusion of the NATO bombing campaign. Equally important, the task force provided some of the initial resources for the U.S. ground units that later entered Kosovo.

Operation ALLIED FORCE ended on 10 June after Slobodan Milosevic agreed to permit NATO peacekeepers to enter Kosovo, while concurrently agreeing to withdraw all Serbian security forces from the province. Formal agreements were quickly signed, reflecting the essence of what had been discussed at Rambouillet (permitting NATO forces to enter Kosovo to restore peace, while also guaranteeing that the province would remain a part of Serbia). To ensure continued security and peace in Kosovo, NATO forces scrambled to deploy their available peacekeepers to the region. Selected personnel from Task Force HAWK provided most of the core American assets that would constitute the initial entry force of the U.S. Army. Changing their designation to Task Force Falcon on 9 June, elements of Hawk began deploying to Camp Able Sentry in Macedonia for insertion the next day into Kosovo as part of Operation Joint Guardian. By 2 August, all Task Force Hawk units had departed from Albania.

Operations

Initial planning for the insertion of a peacekeeping force into Kosovo began in 1998 as conditions in the province steadily deteriorated. At the time, military planners assumed that an agreement similar to the Dayton Accords would be in place prior to a deployment. When the negotiated settlement at Rambouillet collapsed, NATO planners reconsidered the situation, looking at a larger force structure and an entry into the province that might be opposed. Public announcements from the White House and the State Department denied a future commitment of U.S. ground forces in Kosovo, which may have encouraged Milosevic to suffer the air campaign longer than anyone expected. Within USAREUR, however, there were signs suggesting that military personnel would be committed to the province soon, whether there was an agreement or not. The problem was to identify when this commitment would be made and under what circumstances. The diplomatic wrangling and absence of clear guidance forced staff officers to "guess" possible scenarios and then create multiple variations of plans to fit within those exigencies. The extended air campaign against Serbia only added to the uncertainties.

On 1 April 1999, the commander of European Command (EUCOM), General Wesley Clark, directed USAREUR to freeze all planned deployments for organizational training in anticipation of requirements for logistical resources and troop unit moves into Kosovo. Unit training focused on peace enforcement and peacekeeping operations. Concurrently, the Military Traffic Management Command started pre-positioning materiel in Albania, and later in Greece, with one operations officer declaring that Kosovo "has got to be one of the hardest places to get to in the world."

In May, vehicle maintenance became a priority in selected USAREUR organizations, and "it rained mechanics" from other units to ensure that all equipment was fully operational for the U.S. forces scheduled to deploy to Kosovo. Different deployment packages were designed, and some were prepared for shipment by air or sea. As the bombing campaign entered its third month, soldiers found themselves subject to quick recall to their duty stations. By early June, senior commanders were to limit their travel to pre-approved trips for important business. When the battalion com-

Task Organization of Task Force Falcon, June 1999

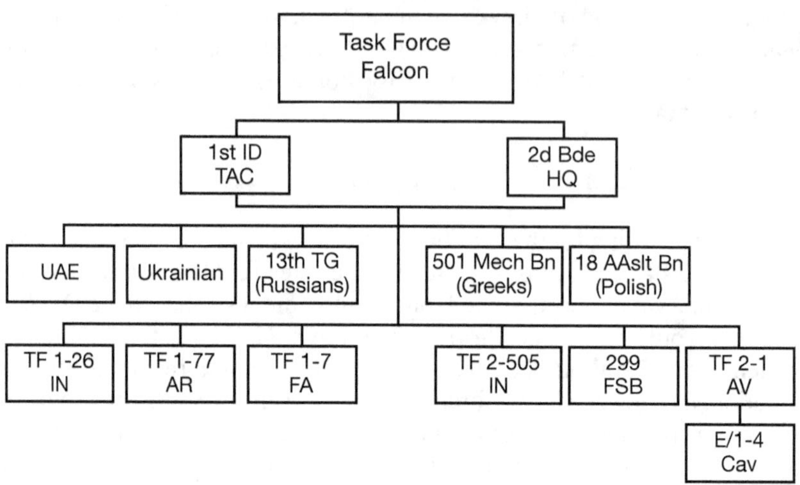

mander for the 1st Battalion, 26th Infantry, received an urgent message while in travel status to report back to his unit within twenty-four hours, it meant only one thing: deployment.

Designated Task Force FALCON (to complement Task Force EAGLE, the avian appellation applied to the U.S. forces in neighboring Bosnia), the peace enforcement operation in Kosovo originally consisted of about thirty-five hundred U.S. personnel. By early spring, this brigade task force doubled in size, with a heavy increment of engineers to lend support in an austere environment. A brigade from the 1st Infantry Division was alerted in early June. By 8 June, the USAREUR task organization for Task Force FALCON, commanded by Brig. Gen. John Craddock, was settled: 1st Battalion, 26th Infantry; 1st Battalion, 77th Armor; 9th Engineer Battalion; 1st Battalion, 7th Field Artillery; 299th Forward Support Battalion; 2d Brigade Reconnaissance Troop; and the headquarters for the 2d Brigade and selected support elements of the 1st Infantry Division.

Getting this force to Kosovo was going to require some time, but the sudden end of the bombing and Serbia's acceptance of NATO peacekeepers in its southern province forced the United States to deploy whatever forces were readily available. The Yugoslav Army was leaving Kosovo, the KLA was quickly moving into the province and asserting its control over communities, and hundreds of thousands of refugees were anxious to return. Although the Serbian security forces were permitted three days to evacuate the province, it quickly became apparent that they would be out of the area much sooner. A small U.S. contingent of fifty-five personnel and twenty vehicles entered Kosovo on 11 June to start securing the designated U.S. zone. To ensure stability in Kosovo and prevent further bloodshed, the United States was able to commit most of the elements from Task Force HAWK, the 26th Marine Expeditionary Unit (MEU), and an advanced contingent from the 1st Infantry Division that was flown in from Germany to Macedonia and then convoyed into Kosovo on 12 June.

NATO divided Kosovo into five multinational brigade sectors: MNB-North (France), MNB-Central (United Kingdom), MNB-West (Italy), MNB-South (Germany), and MNB-East (United States). Within the U.S. sector of KFOR, military personnel from Greece occupied two municipal areas, a combined Polish-Ukrainian unit occupied another municipal area, and a Russian parachute battalion occupied the northern municipal district. U.S. forces in MNB-East held the central sector of three municipal districts, but it would take several days before this precise organizational structure was fully functional.

Operation JOINT GUARDIAN was expected to fulfill a mission with five, basic components:

- Establish a secure presence in Kosovo in accordance with UN Security Council Resolution 1244 and the Military Technical Agreement between NATO and Yugoslavia.
- Verify and enforce the terms of the Military Technical Agreement.
- Establish a safe and secure environment for refugees and displaced persons.
- Establish a secure environment to permit international organizations to operate, interim administrations to function, and humanitarian aid to be delivered.
- Help achieve a self-sustaining, secure environment to transfer public responsibilities to civil authority.

"Safe and secure environment": This phrase was a recurring one throughout the peace enforcement operation in Kosovo. For KFOR, it translated into demilitarizing the KLA, working closely with a variety of civilian agencies and a fledgling provincial government, protecting against the possibility of a sudden and hostile return of Serbian military forces, and—the one objective that seemed to dominate the attention of all NATO forces—providing public safety to everyone residing in Kosovo. Yet each day was filled with incidents that underscored just how difficult and dangerous was this task.

KOSOVO FORCE SECTORS (KFOR)
SERBIA
Kosovo Autonomous Province
May 2002
KFOR Sector Boundary
0
20 Miles
0
20 Kilometers
MONTENEGRO
Rozaj
Leposavic
FRENCH SECTOR
Kosovska Mitrovica
Podujevo
HQ
Istok
ITALIAN SECTOR
Pec
Klina
Pristina
BRITISH SECTOR
Orahovac
Bajram Curri
Dakovica
GERMAN SECTOR
Urosevac
U.S.
CAMP
Prizren
Kacani
Kukes
ALBANIA
MACEDON

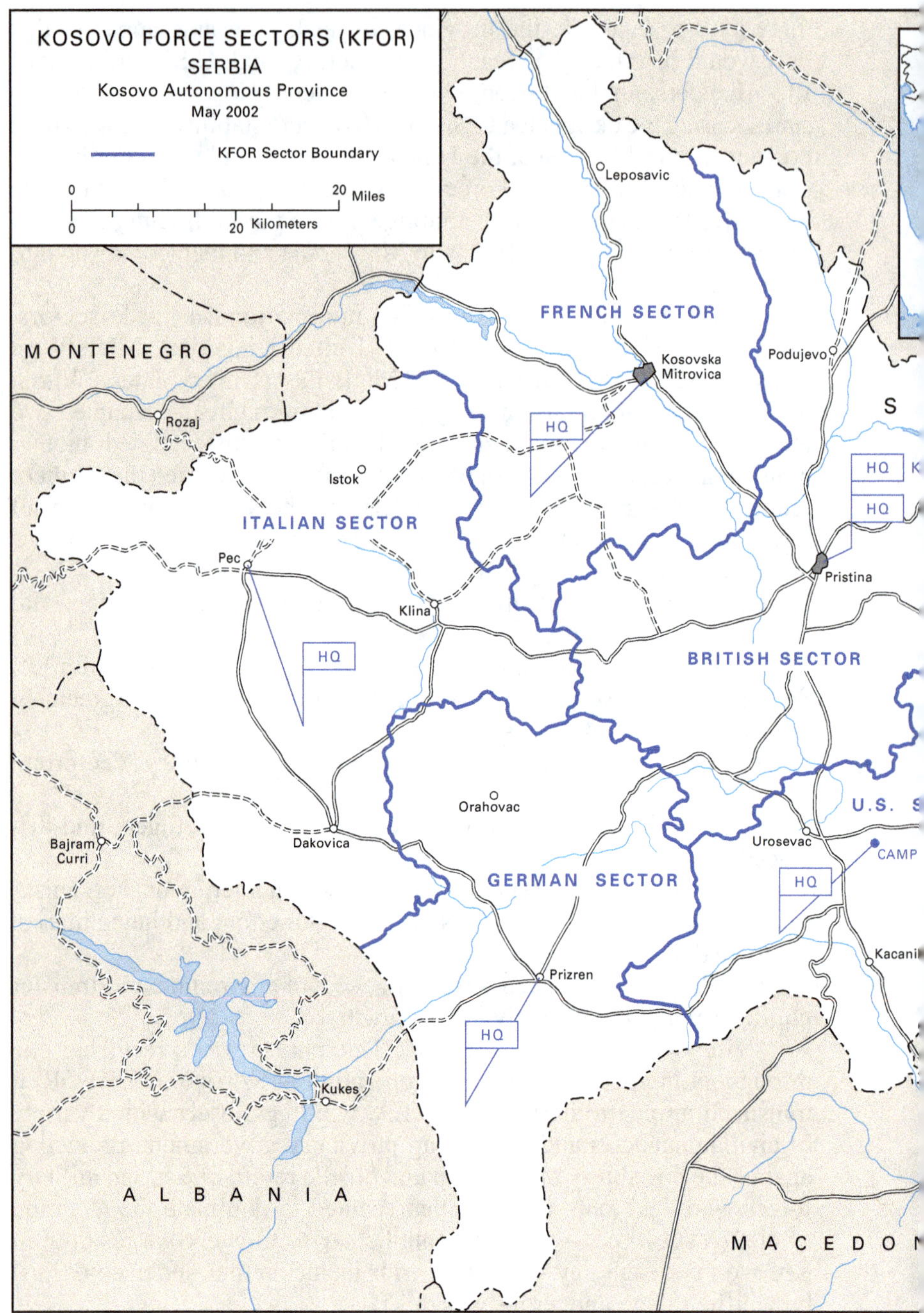

Map 2

Chaos dominated the environment as Operation JOINT GUARDIAN began in earnest. The solitary two-lane road from the Macedonian capital to Kosovo was clogged with refugees and military vehicles, causing five-mile traffic jams that lasted up to six hours. Macedonian border guards exacerbated the situation, and some civilian contract vehicles were delayed entry into Kosovo for as many as five days. In Germany, units and their equipment were intermingled on aircraft to maximize available space, which was an efficient solution to get units in the air en route to Kosovo, but one that added to confusion at the arrival airfield. In spite of these difficulties, within forty-eight hours of the end of the air campaign, there were about two hundred fifty "trigger-pullers" in MNB-East, occupying two campsites (soon to become Camps Bondsteel and Monteith), trying to maintain the peace among more than one hundred and fifty thousand civilians—a number that was growing daily as ethnic Albanian refugees returned to their homes and communities.

No one in Task Force FALCON anticipated the level of violence and lawlessness, sometimes within minutes, following the departure of the Serbian security forces and preceding the arrival of NATO forces. The task force entered the province prepared to protect ethnic Albanians only to discover that the tables had turned: Ethnic Serbs now required the protection. Thousands of Serbs fled Kosovo within days of the end of Operation ALLIED FORCE. One municipality went from a population of ten thousand Serbs to fewer than twenty. Murder, assault, kidnapping, extortion, burglary, and arson were reported daily throughout the province, notwithstanding the vigilance and aggressive patrolling by NATO forces. One Task Force FALCON staff officer summarized the early days of Operation JOINT GUARDIAN well: "I think everybody was surprised at the amount of retribution that was occurring. . . . We handled it the best we could. . . . Short of having a soldier in front of every Serb house, there was no way we were going to stop it."

Many departing Serbs destroyed their own homes and any property that they could not carry out of Kosovo. Animals that could not be taken were slaughtered. One staff officer later reported: "The horizon glowed with burning houses." Abandoned Serbian military installations were destroyed, vandalized, or mined. Even grave sites were booby-trapped. Electricity was intermittent; clean water was almost nonexistent. The absence of order and public services was total.

In the first few hours of the transition, fleeing Serbian civilians and security forces were responsible for most of the property destruction in Kosovo, but the source of destruction soon changed. Ethnic Albanians, consumed with hatred and resolved to avenge past grievances, initiated a wave of destruction that equaled in method if not in volume what they had experienced earlier during the Serbian ethnic cleansing of the province. Anything Serbian was destroyed or vandalized—even abandoned houses and churches. Moreover, much of the violence was clearly organized and deliberate. Each day in June, American soldiers confronted new expressions of hatred. A newborn infant was found abandoned outside the city of Vitina. Reputedly, the mother had been raped by a Serb, and she refused to care for the child. U.S. soldiers placed the baby with an Albanian health clinic.

Sadly, the violence was not confined to isolated incidents or property destruction. Kosovo-Serbs were attacked throughout the province. Even before the first week of KFOR occupation ended, at least twenty-seven ethnic Serbian men were known to have been abducted by members of the KLA. The men were never found. A Serbian school official who had protected an Albanian home and family during the Serbian ethnic cleansing in 1998 thought he would be safe once the war ended in June the following year and Yugoslav forces withdrew. He was not. KLA personnel arrived ahead of NATO's KFOR; they killed the man and his wife and left their bodies hanging in the town square. Other Serbs were accosted in public buildings, or on the street, and then robbed, beaten, or "arrested" and detained in jails for several days. Some of them simply "disappeared." In one community, an estimated five thousand Roma, who had occasionally cooperated with the Serbs during their reign of terror, were expelled from their homes, which were then looted and burned. Muslim Slavs and Albanians who had remained in Kosovo during the Serbian ethnic cleansing often were harassed by returning Albanian refugees, and some of them also disappeared.

What occurred elsewhere in Kosovo happened within the U.S. sector as well. A U.S. Army patrol in MNB-East, while on the lookout for weapons in late June, found a large cache of ammunition in a cave outside a village. In a side chamber of that cave, the patrol also found several corpses of men, women, and children. The available identification indicated that the victims were all Serbs. Other Army patrols confiscated a variety of weapons and ordnance, most of it aged and some of it dating back to World War II. So much was collected in such a short time that it caused a momentary storage and security problem for U.S. forces. Land mines, too, were a pervasive problem throughout MNB-East. Community wells often were polluted with dead bodies, or booby-trapped. U.S. KFOR personnel were kept busy crisscrossing the countryside with each report of gunfire, which usually involved Albanians and Serbs shooting at each other.

A soldier from the 1st Battalion, 77th Armor, stands guard to protect a Serbian church from vandalism or destruction.

Within days of NATO forces arriving in Kosovo, a U.S. Marine patrol in Task Force FALCON responded to a series of home fires in the town of Zegra, near the Kosovo-Macedonian border, but the patrol arrived too late to stop the violence that had engulfed the small community. In a town almost evenly split between Serbian and Albanian families, every Serbian home had been put to the torch. The local church had been destroyed. The cemetery was vandalized. Gunfire was directed at the marines, who returned fire and killed one ethnic Albanian. Almost six hundred Serbs were forced to leave the town.

In the chaotic environment of those first few days, a typical situation unfolded in Gnjilane near the center of MNB-East. On 10 July 1999, several dozen Serbs were spotted milling around an open area by two U.S. KFOR personnel stationed in a tower that overlooked most of the town. While the soldiers' attention was drawn to these Serbs, three heavily

These damaged gravestones are one of the few physical reminders that a Serb village was nearby. Homes, church, and cemetery were completely destroyed.

armed ethnic Albanians suddenly appeared in an alley near the tower. They approached the rear entrance of a Serbian auto-parts store and tried to force their way in. The Serbs inside refused entry to the Albanians, who then started shooting into the store.

The U.S. personnel in the tower turned their attention to the gunfire, reported the incident, and monitored what was happening through a sniper scope. At the same time, a civilian vehicle drove to the front of the store, and its occupant started shooting inside the building. The Albanians saw the soldiers in the tower and fired at them. The soldiers returned fire, killing one of the Albanians. Moments later, a Serbian occupant in the store fired at the soldiers in the tower, and the firefight degenerated, with all three parties shooting at each other. Moments later, an Army patrol arrived to engage the assailants and cordon off the area, while an AH–64 helicopter hovered in the distance. A machine gun on the ground floor of another building fired on the Americans, but U.S. personnel did not engage, because they observed a small child on the floor above the machine-gun position.

Within minutes, the shooting stopped. Three Albanians had been killed, and an undetermined number of Albanians and Serbs were wounded. Seventeen suspects were detained. All of the Albanian suspects eventually were released, but the new Albanian civil authorities insisted on bringing the Serb detainees to trial for murder in spite of statements from the American soldiers concerning the entire fight. As it happened, however, the security system in the Serbian store had recorded the whole episode on videotape. With U.S. KFOR representatives standing by, the tape was shown to the Albanian magistrate, who reluctantly released the Serbian prisoners and dropped the murder charges.

By 10 July, the bulk of the U.S. Army contingent from Europe was in-country. This presence permitted relief for the 26th MEU, which would leave Kosovo. To ensure a seamless transfer of authority, the relief occurred during the early morning darkness. With the entire province under a strict curfew, it is unlikely that anyone was even aware of the change in units. From this point on, the U.S. KFOR mission in MNB-East was largely an Army operation.

On 15 July, during market day in Vitina, a bomb exploded outside a former Serbian store, injuring more than thirty civilians—all ethnic Serbs. A few days later, U.S. KFOR launched a combined ground and air assault at a mine site near Novo Brdo to seize a large quantity of explosives. In spite of careful preparations to ensure surprise, the reinforced rifle company was engaged by KLA personnel. However, the speed of movement and overwhelming firepower of the U.S. forces suppressed the hostile fire. There were no casualties on either side. Seven tons of explosives and thirty-eight hundred blasting caps were confiscated, and eight ethnic Albanians were detained. Similar episodes peppered the daily operations of U.S. KFOR.

Throughout the first month of the peace enforcement operation in the U.S. sector, the level of violence did not change significantly. The daily routine entailed the same jobs: fight fires, disperse crowds, and quell violence. Small caches of weapons and ammunition usually were found every day. Wounded Serbs were treated regularly by Army medics or evacuated to medical facilities at Camps Bondsteel or Monteith. The episodes seemed constant and blended into an endless stream of violence.

It probably was inevitable that there would be some American casualties in such an intense environment. In mid-July, three U.S. soldiers died in two separate incidents. The first combat death, Spc. Benjamin McGill, occurred as he and two fellow soldiers were pursuing armed Albanians who had recently fired at the Americans. McGill adjusted his vehicle antenna moments before it struck a power line, killing him instantly. Two more soldiers died hours later when their armored vehicle skidded off the road and overturned. These men, too, were responding to reports of gunfire at a nearby village.

Although it was not uncommon for U.S. personnel to be fired on by either Albanian or Serbian snipers in Kosovo, assaults on military personnel from other nations in MNB-East were more frequent—and sometimes bolder. The Russian battalion in the northern sector was frequently harassed by ethnic Albanians. During daylight hours, such harassment usually was limited to thrown rocks, blocked traffic, and shouted protests. The evenings, however, would be punctuated with random gunfire and explosions close to Russian checkpoints. In one brazen attack that first summer, a Russian soldier was wounded, and the isolated outpost of Russian soldiers was pelted with rocks until American artillery fired six illumination rounds to light the area and the attackers finally dispersed. The Russians' response to this episode, and to several similar ones, elicited high praise from a U.S. operations officer: "They behaved very well and showed incredible restraint considering the violence."

At the other end of MNB-East, the combined Polish and Ukrainian battalion often tried to protect Serbian homes and churches with stationary guards. In a typical episode in early August, an Albanian mob approached a Serbian home late at night. The KFOR soldiers guarding the site called for reinforcements moments before gunfire erupted between the Serbs in the house and the Albanians outside. The latter group fled as more KFOR soldiers and an AH–64 helicopter arrived on the scene. At least one Albanian was wounded in the fight.

Ethnic Serbs left Kosovo daily. Sometimes entire blocks of Serbian communities would depart, usually under a U.S. KFOR escort to minimize Albanian harassment en route to the Serbian border. Whereas the Serbian ethnic cleansing that preceded Operation JOINT GUARDIAN was well organized and calculated to create massive population relocations, this new Albanian ethnic cleansing was more random and tended to focus on only a few families at a time. Even then, however, there was some predictability in how Kosovo-Albanians bullied their Serbian neighbors to leave the province. Remote villages were especially sensitive to the unofficial pattern, which tended to play out in the following way. By mid-June, often a few Serb families in a given village would have already left for Serbia. If they had not destroyed their own homes before they fled, roving bands of ethnic Albanian youths would do so days later. The presence of the youths and the burning, vacant houses usually caused other Serbs to flee, thus permitting more vacant houses to be set on fire or demolished with explosives. Afterward, the few Serbs still residing in the village—usually older and often completely apolitical—would be subject to intimidation tactics: a broken window, a killed goat, or graffiti scrawled on a garden wall. Typically, the remaining families would depart after such threats became unbearable. If these tactics did not achieve the desired end, however, thugs would break into selected homes and beat the occupants, and one or two token victims would be killed. The process was very effective.

Shortly after the market bombing in Vitina, Albanians began an intimidation campaign against the three Serbian families who still lived in the town, accusing them of being involved in destroying the market square. Officially, the Serbs were cleared of any involvement, but the harassment continued—even though their Albanian neighbors insisted that the Serbian families were innocent. A U.S. Army guard was stationed near the Serbian homes, but apparently did not provide a sufficient sense of security, and the inhabitants abruptly departed for Serbia. Before leaving, the families gave their houses and remaining property to their Albanian neighbors in gratitude for their friendship and kindness. The neighbors never had an opportunity to take possession of the property. With the departure of the Serbian families, the Army guard was removed. That evening all three houses and the property inside were destroyed by fire, leading a U.S. Army battalion commander to laconically observe: "The hatred is so intense and irrational it is unbelievable."

Serbs who remained in Kosovo often banded together in tighter enclaves, surrounded as they were by ethnic Albanians. This tactic provided some measure of security, but it also imposed restrictions on movement outside such enclaves. In the countryside, among farmers, the situation was equally troublesome. Serbs were afraid to venture out to their fields for fear of being shot or harassed. In the few remaining areas where ethnic Albanians were the minority, a similar fear and paralysis prevailed. In mixed communities, Albanians and Serbs rarely went out to their fields to tend their crops.

The phenomenon was symptomatic of a larger one, which American military personnel simply could not comprehend: the depth and breadth of hatred and anger that infected virtually all natives of Kosovo. Other Western European countries were equally baffled by the Albanian-Serbian intransigence, which extended to Kosovo's intelligentsia. Serbian and Albanian writers, journalists, and other intellectuals proclaimed their resolute animosity to each other and categorical refusal to be reconciled. Exasperated by repeated frustration in getting Albanians and Serbs to talk to each other without shouting and to work together without fighting, one battalion commander was led to plaintively sigh: "Can't we just all get along?" But in those first weeks of Operation JOINT

GUARDIAN, any getting along could only happen in the armed presence of U.S. KFOR peacekeepers—and even then it was almost impossible to stop the violence.

In one typical Albanian-majority Kosovo village, U.S. KFOR personnel were able to arrange for farmers to alternate days in which they would tend their crops. The plan lasted less than a week before an elderly Serbian farmer was shot in the back of his head while returning from his fields. Recriminations sailed back and forth, but the murderer was never found. In a standard refrain, no one saw anything. A U.S. KFOR unit launched a surprise raid on the village, which uncovered a few weapons caches and nothing more. Two more Serbs were killed two weeks later, and then snipers fired random shots at a nearby U.S. patrol. It was enough to persuade the remaining two hundred Serbs in the village to flee; half went to Serbia, and the other half joined other Serbian enclaves in Kosovo. Within seventy-two hours, all the abandoned Serbian property had been looted and the houses destroyed.

Even if it seemed that the Army had made little headway during the first two months of Operation JOINT GUARDIAN, significant changes actually had occurred and conditions in Kosovo had improved however slowly. The most obvious element of success was the absence of massive ethnic cleansing of Kosovo-Albanians. Unfortunately, the reverse was happening to Kosovo-Serbs, albeit on a much smaller scale and level of intensity. Progress in rebuilding the province, restoring its economy, and repairing its infrastructure was still months away, but the wholesale destruction of homes and businesses was being stopped. By the end of August, statistics for MNB-East indicated that the level of violence was declining. Comparing the first three weeks of August with the last week of the month, the number of reported assaults dropped almost in half. Only one-third the number of kidnappings was reported, and there were no murders, whereas fifteen killings had been reported during the first three weeks of the month. When contrasted with the hundreds of murders, assaults, and kidnappings that preceded the arrival of KFOR three months earlier, this reduction in violence was no mean achievement.

Although the suppression of further acts of violence would continue to require considerable effort on the part of the soldiers of Task Force FALCON, it soon became apparent that they would need to tackle other criminal activities and lawless elements as well. Smuggling, prostitution, and drug trafficking beleaguered the province. Albanians even stole relief supplies designated for other Albanians and tried to sell the stolen goods on the black market. Such thefts led to speculation that not all the violence in Kosovo was ethnically motivated—though certainly the most violent crimes were. The overarching concern of U.S. KFOR personnel remained nonetheless to create a safe and secure environment, whether that meant soldiers laboring to prevent murders and assaults driven by ethnic hatred, or to intercept contraband or drugs smuggled for profit. In either case, Task Force FALCON kept busy.

Civic action initiatives and humanitarian assistance eased some of the discomfort that the civilian population suffered, even as it mitigated some of the criminal activity in an oblique sort of way. If Kosovars had jobs, public services, and a sense of responsibility for their respective communities, so the thinking went, they would be less likely to engage in vandalism, robbery, smuggling, tax evasion, or other criminal activities. Charitable agencies and international nongovernmental organizations (NGOs) provided most of the humanitarian assistance, but U.S. Army battalions and companies also distributed food and clothing to Kosovars, which military installations in the United States and Germany donated. In 1999, for example, one company collected 4,500 pairs of shoes and distributed them to Kosovar children in the U.S. area of operations.

In turn, Task Force FALCON often provided the NGOs and other relief agencies with security and helped to coordinate or facilitate their operations within MNB-East. Usually, U.S. KFOR personnel and units were the only ones who had sufficient resources available to bring (sometimes compel) ethnic Albanians and Serbs to meet in the same room at the same time with an NGO representative who might be trying to arrange for the restoration of public utilities or the reopening of a local school.

Army engineers invested thousands of hours in repairing or rebuilding public schools in response to the damage or destruction of almost five hundred educational facilities throughout the province between 1996 and 1999. In some cases, reconstruction and repairs were delayed because rival ethnic groups had salted school property with land mines or booby traps. Building supplies were sparse, and school supplies were almost nonexistent.

In response, individual Army units took it upon themselves to solicit their home stations, and, in less than twelve months, received hundreds of pounds of school supplies, including writing instruments, paper, and notebooks, which they distributed to schoolchildren in MNB-East. Some U.S. KFOR personnel arranged for school partnerships, with American students corresponding with Kosovar students. Other military personnel wrote to U.S. corporations asking for donations of materials and other supplies. One firm donated six hundred baseball caps to one school alone.

U.S. Army personnel distribute school supplies, winter clothes, and mine-awareness packages to Albanian children in a small town in MNB-East.

Medical missions were common and urgent in war-ravaged Kosovo. Within weeks of the arrival of Task Force FALCON, medical personnel determined that twenty-one of twenty-nine municipalities in MNB-East were infected by tularemia, a bacterial disease usually found in food and water contaminated by dead animals and spread by rodents. At least one medical or dental civic action program emanated from Task Force FALCON every week.

Sadly, not all civic action initiatives were completely successful. In one battalion area in mid-August, Army personnel tried to encourage both Albanian and Serbian farmers to work together to harvest the wheat crop in their community. They were offered an incentive of free fuel for their tractors and combines in what the Army dubbed Operation HARVEST. Among the farmers, few Serbs and even fewer Albanians were willing to participate. On the day the fuel was to be distributed, it became clear that the amount was insufficient to accommodate all the program participants, even though they were few in number. The Serbian farmers protested and abruptly withdrew from the harvest. After extensive negotiations, a feeble compromise resulted in the fuel being divided equally between the two ethnic groups, who would harvest their crops on alternate days. The effort was judged to be a partial success: The wheat crop was harvested (generating food and income for the community), and no one was killed.

Efforts to stimulate the economy and rebuild the region in municipal areas were equally frustrating—and only partially successful. Initially, command guidance was to encourage proportional representation in the workforce. Thus, large businesses were to have a roughly two-to-one Albanian-Serbian labor force. The imposition of this form of affirmative action rarely worked. Serbs consistently insisted that they should return to their former managerial positions occupied in the 1990s. The majority Albanians, meanwhile, demanded their jobs from a decade earlier. A legacy of forty years of socialism compounded the problem, with some workers insisting on being paid regardless of the quality or quantity of work performed. Denied their former managerial positions of authority and fearful for their own safety, few Serbs ventured outside their municipal enclaves to work in factories or larger businesses in Kosovo. Ultimately, U.S. KFOR personnel accepted any solution that generated business activity, which usually meant commercial enterprises run and staffed exclusively by Albanians.

In view of the limited mobility of Serbs in the U.S. sector of Kosovo, a battalion launched an effort in late August to ensure that public transportation was available in both Serbian and Albanian neighborhoods. Given the evocative nickname Operation ROSA PARKS, armed guards periodically monitored bus stops and routes and rode on buses to ensure the safety of all patrons. In spite of high hopes and a festive beginning, the project ended in less than two weeks. Few Albanians would ride the buses into Serbian neighborhoods, and no Serbs would ride the buses at all. The Serbs feared trouble more than isolation.

Traditionally, most schools were completely segregated in Kosovo. In ethnically mixed communities, each population usually had its own separate school, though the Albanian one usually was under-resourced. Occasionally, the two ethnic groups made use of the same building, with Albanian schoolchildren attending at one time of the day and Serbian schoolchildren at another. Both "schools" had separate teachers, administrators, and materials. The ethnic cleansing, which the Serbs conducted in the 1990s had a profound impact on Albanian education. As the Serbian reign of terror began in earnest, most Albanian children were expelled from their schools and Albanian school buildings were destroyed.

Once the United Nations Mission in Kosovo (UNMIK) established itself as the principal international civilian agency administering affairs in the province, it directed all schools in Kosovo to reopen by 15 September 1999. Although agencies outside of Kosovo insisted on meeting the prescribed deadline, and doing so with fully integrated schools and classes, U.S. KFOR personnel accepted a more realistic time line and solutions. Every effort was made to make the school buildings habitable and operational by mid-September. Most teachers worked without salaries until December; there were few textbooks and no school supplies, except for the small contributions coming from American soldiers. Schoolchildren and teachers often were the Army personnel's greatest supporters, and they frequently greeted the irregular visits as festive occasions. Recognizing that these children represented the next generation of Kosovars, U.S. KFOR personnel consciously used these lighter moments to stress the need to break the cycle of hatred and violence that saturated the province. Their efforts, of course, led to no quick or easy changes of heart.

Schools in ethnically mixed communities posed the greatest problem, and in a number of incidents revealed just how intense the hatred was that divided Kosovo. In Vitina, where Albanians outnumbered Serbs two to one, the minority Serbs categorically refused to send their children to integrated schools—even when promised military escorts and security on school grounds. And in a small village, where Serbs lived surrounded by a larger, rural community of ethnic Albanians, the former refused to permit the latter to attend its school. When the Albanians demanded access to the facility, a representative of a U.S. civilian agency encouraged them to press their demands. With no compromise or negotiation in sight, U.S. military personnel escorted twenty Albanian students and their teacher to the outskirts of the village on 6 October 1999, where a Serbian mob blocked the road and entrance to the school. Led by their parish priest, the Serbs threw rocks and adamantly refused to yield. Realizing that children could be injured if the issue were pressed further, the U.S. commander on the ground backed down and withdrew the Albanian students.

Elsewhere in the U.S. area of operations, some mixed schools functioned—albeit in a quasi-integrated environment. Usually in such cases, Albanian schoolchildren attended classes in one part of a school building while Serb students attended classes in another—all at the same time. An armed security detail from Task Force Falcon kept the peace between the two groups of learners, as well as their teachers, whom one Army officer sardonically characterized as "school moms with M–16s."

In another time and place, such an arrangement might not have been impressive; but given that Operation Joint Guardian had only been in place for a few weeks, the outcome actually did show progress. At least children were back in school, receiving a rudimentary education, and were no longer subject to the violence that had terrified them months earlier. Looking back on the first few weeks of that new school year, one U.S. KFOR officer proudly proclaimed, "There's hope."

Although the statistics suggested a decline in crime, individual episodes continued to bedevil U.S. KFOR. In Vitina, a woman was beaten in her home, and her son was shot and killed. A convoy of families fleeing to Serbia was attacked outside an Albanian village, and, in the melee that followed, one Serb was wounded and an Albanian was killed. More Serbian houses were burned and weapons caches discovered in MNB-East. A Serbian woman and her two-year-old daughter were shot and wounded near Gnjilane. The next day, another mother and her four-year-old child were wounded; the mother later died of her wounds before medical personnel could reach her. Protests and vandalism erupted outside two Kosovo villages, with one group taunting a Russian KFOR outpost and another group complaining about the detention of ten ethnic Albanians who had hidden a large weapons cache. These incidents were not the only ones to occur in MNB-East during a typical week in August. They were the incidents "significant" enough to report.

The KLA continued to challenge KFOR restrictions on firearms, political activities, and public assemblies. When U.S. KFOR personnel raided a KLA headquarters in August, documents were found that indicated the organization was engaged in kidnapping and the creation of forged confessions from local Serbs. Other documents authenticated the KLA kidnapping and beating of an Albanian woman simply because her father had been a policeman employed by Serbs years earlier. The raid also revealed information about a large weapons cache and a clandestine KLA training facility in Gnjilane. Days later, U.S. KFOR personnel raided the site, seizing a variety of mines, firearms, and explosives and detaining seventy suspects.

The site of the raid became tense when a large crowd formed around the U.S. KFOR personnel before their prisoners could be evacuated and the confiscated materiel secured. Small groups of protesters rushed the Americans, knocking down four soldiers and kicking them before their comrades could pull them away. As another group started to rush the U.S. commander, the latter leveled his pistol at their apparent leader and ordered the group to halt. The attackers froze, as a chorus of clicks from the Americans indicated that their rifles were being readied for

This modified Albanian national flag was used by the KLA. Public display of these flags was not permitted in Kosovo, and this one was seized during a U.S. raid on a KLA headquarters near Gnjilane in August 1999. The flag is on display at the National Infantry Museum, Fort Benning, Georgia.

engagement. Moments later, a detachment of Military Police with guard dogs arrived to help disperse the crowd. Additional personnel, armored vehicles, and helicopters sped to the scene as the crowd melted away. In spite of the deliberate provocation, only the training and courage of the entire U.S. KFOR unit kept this situation from spinning out of control and altering the entire Kosovo mission. Maj. Steve Russell, an operations officer who was in the thick of the situation, later wrote: "Thank God for the discipline of our soldiers."

Controlling large, hostile crowds was never easy because of so many variables that might influence a particular situation. Also dominating each confrontation was the awareness on the part of Kosovars—whether Albanian or Serbian—that Americans would resort to deadly force only in extreme emergencies or after all other options had been exhausted. Thus in the raid at the KLA training facility when U.S. military personnel deliberately prepared their weapons to be fired, the crowd quickly realized that the threat was no idle one. The situation was only seconds away from becoming a deadly confrontation.

There were, however, other means of influencing and muting crowd behavior. Sometimes such methods might be carefully orchestrated, as when a local KLA leader and his minions thought they could defy U.S. personnel and not surrender a cache of weapons or abide by the KFOR curfew during that first summer of Operation Joint Guardian. An Army officer with a small patrol in tow advised the KLA chieftain and his followers to cooperate, or else U.S. KFOR would simply replace them. Suddenly, a flight of three AH–64 Apache helicopters zoomed overhead to punctuate the point. It "scared the hell out of the Albanians," and KFOR had no more trouble from these KLA personnel.

Such a show of force proved to be the right tactic to mitigate a situation that could have quickly become violent. U.S. military personnel soon learned that ethnic Albanians tended to regard any armored vehicle as a formidable tank. Thus, even the employment of an M2 Bradley infantry fighting vehicle could intimidate an angry crowd. There were limitations. Albanians also realized that Americans would not run over or through crowds with a "tank." Thus many protesters would simply surround an armored vehicle and sit down. In one such case in early August, a large crowd started throwing debris at and threatening the dismounted soldiers. This time, two soldiers, on their own initiative, removed a large roll of concertina wire from their Bradley and proceeded to unwind it in an expanding line away from the U.S. forces and toward the protesters, which forced the crowd to back away and thin out as they became further separated from the Americans. The U.S. commander then invited the leader of the protest to meet him in the open area that separated them. As the negotiations dragged on, the evening curfew approached, and all but the most committed went to their homes. The few that remained after the curfew were quickly rounded up and detained by U.S. KFOR personnel.

When crowds were smaller and less belligerent, it was not uncommon for an Army leader to ask for three spokesmen to come forward to air their grievances. When the spokesmen came forward, the soldier would slowly walk them away from the crowd, ideally to an open area, where the protesters were likely to follow and eventually disperse. The tactic also helped identify the leadership among the protesters. A bolder approach to managing belligerent crowds involved an Army leader peacefully walking through the protesters in the opposite direction in which they were headed. The soldier might be "roughed up," but the tactic usually stopped the forward movement of the crowd and often turned it around completely. Surprisingly, before a crowd became unruly, the least harmless, but most potent deterrent among protesters in Kosovo was the digital camera. Few wanted their pictures taken, especially the more vocal among them and their leaders.

By late summer, Task Force FALCON started using public service announcements to address larger issues affecting the safety of Kosovars in MNB-East. A chronic problem was the pervasive presence of mines and unexploded ordnance. The seriousness of the situation was highlighted in mid-August, when a father and his two daughters went swimming in a local pond. The water disturbed a bomb that exploded, killing the father and one daughter and injuring the other daughter. When the man's sister visited the site the next day, she saw a shiny metal object and picked it up. It, too, was a bomb, which exploded and killed the woman. Local radio broadcasts produced by KFOR personnel repeatedly advised civilians to avoid touching anything that looked suspicious.

Local radio broadcasts also provided the Army with opportunities to stress the need to change attitudes among Kosovars and encourage more civil multiethnic relations. Throughout the summer, short, direct vignettes addressed a variety of community concerns that ranged from driving safely to rebuilding homes, as well as valuing human life and showing kindness and respect for others. Often presented as a dialog between two fictional local residents, each vignette ended with the narrator stating, "This is a generation for peace. Start now!" Although it is arguable how effective these measures were in mitigating either the volume or the intensity of violence that inflamed the region, the broadcasts clearly underscored the Army's efforts to engage every possible resource to stop the ethnic conflict in MNB-East.

As the first summer of the operation drew to a close, a brief lull in the violence came to an abrupt end. Mortar rounds were fired, usually at night, in the vicinity of Serbian dwellings, and hand grenades were thrown from speeding cars or lobbed over garden walls. From safe distances, rocket-propelled grenades and short bursts of machine-gun fire were directed at U.S. KFOR patrols. Military authorities regarded these incidents as ominous signs of a lack of concern about the KFOR response. The acts of violence directed at U.S. military personnel produced no casualties, but the response to each provocation was to "pile-on" more U.S. forces in the area of engagement. The surge in violence soon abated, however, and constant vigilance ensured that the challenges to KFOR authority remained in check throughout the year.

During the first four months that Operation JOINT GUARDIAN had been in place in the heavily patrolled U.S. sector of MNB-East, there were 40 hostile-fire incidents, 11 mortar attacks, 3 hand grenade attacks, 3 mine strikes, and 7 riots. The operational tempo through the remainder of the year did not change significantly, and only with some hindsight were KFOR personnel able to affirm that some progress was being made.

Random terror attacks continued, with the hand grenade serving as the "weapon of choice." Walled yards and garden areas and homes that abutted narrow, winding streets facilitated the use of these explosives. Moreover, hand grenades were both plentiful and inexpensive, costing about $7.50 each—less than the price of a pound of coffee in Kosovo. A single hand grenade in a car or truck was one of the most common pieces of ordnance confiscated at KFOR roadblocks and checkpoints. On the eve of one battalion's redeployment back to Germany in December and following a spate of grenade attacks in which there were "no witnesses," the unit historian summarized the sentiments of his fellow soldiers, who were becoming "disgusted with the complete lack of a civilized nature or sense of morality among the people."

Near the end of 1999, the original U.S. military units that had come to Kosovo began to rotate out of the region, with new organizations making a smooth transition into their peace-enforcement mission. One newly arrived unit received an early introduction to the entrenched hatred in Kosovo when in late November a routine patrol found an infant, barely two hours old and of mixed ethnicity, abandoned on a trash pile. Medical personnel were able to save the baby, whom an Albanian family later adopted. In another incident, on the eve of the Christmas season, a car sped through a town in MNB-East and sprayed machine gun fire on a Serbian girl walking down the street. She was seriously wounded, but U.S. medical personnel saved her life as well.

And so the pattern continued. Each incident told its own story of fear and terror, human misery and depravation, hatred and violence. Throughout the remainder of 1999 and continuing into 2000, no Army report or briefing, nor personal reminiscence by individual commanders and staff officers, could avoid citing episodes of murder, arson, or vandalism. Yet two characteristics soon became apparent nonetheless. First, the reported acts of violence became less frequent and affected fewer people. Certainly murders and assaults on minorities still occurred in 2000, but now they were reported on a weekly basis and no longer were the daily events that dominated the early summer of 1999. Second, crowds could gather in municipal areas in 2000 without always starting a riot, and phrases such as "celebrated peacefully" and "without violence" began to appear in various reports. At last the long-sought safe and secure environment that underscored the mission of Operation JOINT GUARDIAN had begun to take hold in Kosovo. KFOR vigilance was having an effect on the region. At the same time, of course, the diminished violence could be attributed to the fact that fewer ethnic Serbs resided in the province than ever before.

2000 Onward

By the start of the new millennium, a large collection of civil affairs assessments had been completed, which provided some direction for anticipated long-range projects. The data did not reveal anything that was not already apparent: jobs, clean water, winter clothing, and food dominated civilian needs. Some communities were 100 percent unemployed. The data also identified the areas most severely affected by the war. Coupled with its mission to respond to such basic human needs was Task Force FALCON's resolve to give the mixed-ethnic communities the highest priority.

By 2000, UNMIK was adequately staffed at local levels to assume many of the civil administrative responsibilities that had fallen on Task Force FALCON in the early days of Operation JOINT GUARDIAN. Clearly, UNMIK would have more than enough to do: promote the commercial development of the province, rebuild the economy, oversee local elections, develop a civilian police force, and generally improve the quality of life for all Kosovars. It was obvious, however, that KFOR would remain in the province for several more years. To even the casual observer, Kosovo was a powder keg: One little incident could spark other crises that might lead to a major disruption. Even with the diminished level of violence, plenty of incidents threatened to disrupt the peace that U.S. forces had worked so hard to enforce and now tried to maintain.

On 9 January 2000, an elderly man was shot outside his home while cutting firewood. Four weeks later another elderly man was shot and killed when he opened his front door to receive a visitor. Both men were Serbs—life-long residents in the community. In the same municipal district and on 26 February, a Serb surgeon, his wife, and three children were murdered outside their home, prompting several dozen Kosovo-Serbian families to flee for the safety of Serbia. One Serb lingered in the community and tried to sell his home; he was killed in April by an Albanian masquerading as a potential buyer. Ethnic Serbs were not the only victims. A local Albanian, who had worked for Serbian security forces four years earlier, was killed while on an errand for a friend. None of the murderers was captured. In the first four months of 2000, U.S. KFOR personnel seized in that same district sixteen hand grenades, eight firearms, and more than a thousand rounds of ammunition.

The number of murder victims that season, however, was notably lower than what had been customary in almost any single month the previous year. The volume of ordnance that was confiscated was equally unremarkable. It was disappointing, therefore, that more Serbs continued to leave Kosovo, as their exodus only tended to reinforce the intimidation tactics of some ethnic Albanians. Despite progress, the troubling aspect of this peace-enforcement mission remained the fact that the violence was continuing—and only the constant vigilance of armed peacekeepers prevented the situation from getting worse.

After almost one year of Operation JOINT GUARDIAN, Task Force FALCON recorded nearly one thousand hostile-fire incidents or attacks (15 percent of them from hand grenades alone) and sixty-three mine strikes. In MNB-East, one KFOR peacekeeper had been killed (a Russian paratrooper) and thirty-two others wounded (twenty-four were Americans). There were five accidental deaths among allied KFOR peacekeepers in MNB-East and three accidental deaths among U.S. KFOR personnel. The number of checkpoints had almost doubled in the past year, and the number of daily security patrols had increased by 14 percent. More than $3.7 million had been spent on various humanitarian assistance projects in the region—not including individual gifts and assistance from American soldiers or materiel provided to Army units from family members and U.S. communities. More than ten thousand pieces of unexploded ordnance had been destroyed in MNB-East since June 1999, and 96 of 158 known minefields had been neutralized by May 2000. The continuing violence within Kosovo, the porous borders, organized crime, and the potential for an increase in insurgent activity kept Task Force FALCON vigilant through 2000.

Attendant to the internal strife that beleaguered Kosovo were concerns regarding Serbia's long-term intentions. Slobodan Milosevic was still in power, but the country was in a state of considerable political turmoil. In the past, Milosevic had succeeded in turning attention away from himself by rallying Serbs to respond militarily to perceived threats to their national security or to prevent the loss of Serbian territory. Not realizing at the time how politically weak the Serbian leader had become, the U.S. KFOR leadership kept a constant eye on activities across the Kosovo border in anticipation of a possible Serbian attack. Although such a scenario never materialized, the possibility did continue to command some concern among American and European military leaders. Vocal demands for complete independence from Serbia made by more extreme ethnic Albanians did not ease their worries.

In spite of the apparent threat from Serbia to the north, border clashes along the Kosovo-Macedonian border often commanded more attention. A typical episode in late summer of 2000 involved a rifle company from the 2d Battalion of the 327th Infantry. Two ethnic Albanians claimed that they had been shot at by Macedonian border guards and that the Albanians' tractor had been abandoned when they fled the gunfire. A patrol sent to the site found several shell casings in the vicinity of the damaged tractor and the trailer it was towing. The soldiers surmised that the Albanians were involved in an illegal woodcutting operation (a common occurrence in the area, which KFOR personnel were trying to curtail) and that the Macedonians had scared them away. Moments later, a Macedonian patrol arrived and challenged the Americans to lower their weapons and depart. Instead, the American patrol leader suggested that both sides lower their weapons and that the leaders meet in the open space between them to discuss the situation. The Macedonians complied, and the American lieutenant used his map to explain that the Macedonians were at least 800 meters inside Kosovo. The Macedonians left the area, and the U.S. patrol removed the battery from the tractor and brought the undamaged trailer back to the Albanians.

Many similar incidents occurred throughout the summer and into the autumn, usually involving illegal woodcutting operations. Wood was a principal source of residential fuel, particularly in rural areas. Although Kosovars were anxious to stockpile as much as possible before the onset of the colder winter months, UNMIK and KFOR were trying to ensure that resources were carefully managed and that the environment was not permanently damaged. The U.S. Army did not routinely patrol border areas because of the tense and uncertain boundaries and unwanted showdowns with Macedonian security forces. Ethnic Albanians exploited the absence of KFOR personnel, and some were wounded or lost property when Macedonian border guards discovered the Albanians. It was simply another flashpoint in a volatile Balkan province.

Late in 2000, after Operation JOINT GUARDIAN had been in place for eighteen months, a prominent, and moderate, Albanian politician was murdered. It appeared that more radical Albanian nationalists, who were seeking independence from Serbia, were involved. In a routine patrol in October near the Kosovo-Serbian border in MNB-East, U.S. KFOR personnel stumbled upon a shepherd's shack in a field. Booby traps surrounded the dwelling, and inside the shelter two ethnic Albanians quickly surrendered. The site also yielded seven rifles and thousands of rounds of ammunition. As the Americans left the scene, they were ambushed by a band of smugglers. No Americans were injured; two of the smugglers were killed, and the others may have escaped across the border into Serbia. Days later, ten armed ethnic Albanians were caught infiltrating the border. A few weeks after their capture, a joint American-Russian patrol in the same vicinity was fired on by a band of men, who also fled back into Serbia before they could be caught.

Yet, for a brief space of time, something other than internecine violence took center stage in the province. The Kosovo municipal elections, held on 28 October, were the first free ones in more than eight years and represented a milestone in both Operation JOINT GUARDIAN and the history of the province. However hopeful and salutary these elections were, they set up many hurdles that UNMIK and KFOR had to overcome—not the least of which was how to manage the large crowds that assembled before the polls opened. Some Kosovars stood in line for six hours in order to exercise their right to vote, and there were difficulties with voter illiteracy and a slow registration process. The gravest problem, however, was not a logistical one. It was the determined absence of Serbs from the polls.

Thus, in the Serb-majority town of Strpce, the newly elected municipal leader—the individual who would wield the greatest influence over the management of city services and the disbursement of local resources—was an ethnic Albanian, as were his municipal staff. The town's Serbian citizens complained bitterly about this electoral development and categorically refused to acknowledge that their absence from the polls had facilitated the outcome. Weeks later, a major civil disturbance erupted when the Albanian mayor moved into the town to occupy its municipal offices. In the meantime, however, the generally peaceful election throughout the province was a welcome respite.

As Task Force FALCON labored to enforce the peace in MNB-East, it also needed to prevent incursions that would disrupt the peace in the southern Balkans. Lingering acts of violence and constant pressure on both ethnic Serbs and moderate Albanians in Kosovo kept U.S. forces fully engaged. At the same time, violence erupted in border areas involving Serbia to the north and east and Macedonia to the south. Later intelligence revealed that radical groups of ethnic Albanians were committed to violence in Kosovo, with the ultimate goal of achieving complete independence from Serbia and bringing along as well bits of territory in Serbia and Macedonia still dominated by ethnic Albanians.

One of the distinct characteristics of the American soldiers in MNB-East was their ability to operate in small groups with minimal oversight, enabling company-grade officers and noncommissioned officers to function with considerable independence. This combination of self-control and resourcefulness was aptly demonstrated in early April 2001 during a routine patrol in the city of Vitina, when a squad leader was alerted to the possible presence of an Albanian terrorist in his area. On his own initiative, the sergeant entered an Albanian café to ask the owner if he had seen anyone matching the description of the terrorist. Although the owner claimed to know nothing, the sergeant noticed a man, seated among seven other patrons, who fit the description of the sought-after individual. When the man could not answer general questions about the local neighborhood, the squad leader asked for his identification. When the man provided a birth date that did not match what was recorded on his identification papers, the sergeant directed one of his soldiers to advise other members of the squad outside the café to be alert for trouble and to call for civilian police from UNMIK. Then he asked the Albanian to step outside.

The other patrons became unruly, shouting obscenities and threatening to intervene. Noticing a bulge under the suspect's jacket, the sergeant and another soldier lifted the man from his seat. As the soldier guided the man out of the café, the squad leader called for reinforcements from his battalion. Once out in the street, the suspect suddenly bolted, pushing the soldiers aside as he ran away. The squad gave pursuit. When the suspect turned down an alley, the squad leader and one soldier followed him while the other five members of the squad took an alternate route to intercept the fleeing Albanian. Several times, the soldiers called on the man to halt. Suddenly, the suspect stopped, turned, and pointed a pistol at his pursuers. But a soldier fired first, wounding the suspect, who then ran down another street, throwing his firearm inside a passing car before running into an abandoned building. The squad circled the building. Minutes later, UNMIK police arrived, found the wounded man inside, and arrested him.

By mid-2001, both smuggling and signs of an insurgent campaign were escalating in the province, particularly in the mountainous and heavily wooded border areas that separated Macedonia and Kosovo. Perhaps smugglers seized the opportunity to exploit the fact that the U.S. KFOR had skirted the border to avoid exacerbating an already tense situation. In any case, it was unfortunate that the wave of contraband entering Kosovo was not confined to illicit drugs or tax-free cigarettes. All too common were the firearms and ordnance among the illegal commodities that crossed these remote mountain paths and roads. By dint of constant effort over the past two years, Task Force FALCON had succeeded in reducing the quantity of firearms within MNB-East, which in turn clearly had reduced the frequency and deadliness of ethnic strife. Now those gains were threatened.

To counter the smuggling operations, Task Force FALCON launched a series of aggressive measures, beginning in the summer of 2001, to stem the flow of weapons entering the province. A common tactic that U.S. forces employed entailed the concealed placement of small patrols at known entry points inside the Kosovo border. Often, smugglers would send a party ahead of the contraband and use cell phones to alert their compatriots behind them of any KFOR patrols in the area. The U.S. personnel would allow such an advance party to pass unchallenged and intercept the second, larger body of smugglers, who carried the weapons or illegal materiel. Meanwhile, a quick reaction force (QRF), alerted by the U.S. Army patrol earlier, would go after the smugglers' advance party.

Some of these smuggling ventures entailed convoys of as many as seven sport utility vehicles fully loaded with contraband. The narrow dirt roads, which were little more than wide paths, could be easily navigated by these vehicles; but, in the rugged terrain, there often was no room to change direction or move fast—even when confronted by soldiers on foot. These interdiction operations confiscated large quantities of drugs, military supplies, and money, and uncovered intelligence data concerning other smuggling operations, as well as the activities of the "Albanian National Liberation Army"—a relatively new creation that threatened the future peace of Kosovo. Such interdiction proved successful. By September 2001, all smuggling activities along the Kosovo-Macedonian border in MNB-East had virtually ceased. In November, the neighboring Vitina district experienced not one bombing, shooting, grenade attack, or act of arson—criminal activities that had occurred almost daily two years earlier. The sudden absence of violence was attributed to the success of the border interdiction campaign. The flow of contraband into Kosovo shifted outside the control of Task Force FALCON. Eventually, the flow was stemmed in those border regions as well.

Smuggling operations did, of course, continue to exist throughout Kosovo, albeit on a much smaller scale, and soon even returned to MNB-East—usually involving one- and two-mule teams traversing mountain paths. By this time, however, Task Force FALCON already had dotted the border areas with platoon-size bases and observation posts that monitored all movements. Aggressive patrolling and careful placement of sensors effectively stemmed the illegal activities of these ethnically identified armed groups—the newest being the "Macedonian Liberation

Army," whose units usually comprised young ethnic-Albanian males from Kosovo.

On main thoroughfares, meanwhile, smugglers found that the tactics used earlier in the mountains could work here as well: An advance party in a small car would precede a larger vehicle by several minutes. Using a cell phone, the smugglers would alert the companion vehicle carrying contraband of any KFOR checkpoints or patrols along the route. Realizing that most vehicle checkpoints were effective only for about twenty minutes, Task Force FALCON adopted a mobile system that permitted aerial surveillance of vehicular traffic and quick shifts in checkpoints. Any suspicious vehicle would be identified, and then a team of soldiers would be air assaulted into a prearranged location to establish a hasty checkpoint and intercept the targeted vehicle. It was an effective gambit that the smugglers could not circumvent.

As summer 2001 came to an end, Task Force FALCON had developed a regular rotation of deployments, with fresh battalions entering Kosovo every six months to replace organizations that had served a six-month tour. Specific mission-readiness exercises (MREs) prepared the units for their tasks in Kosovo, and these exercises often focused on the most serious circumstances that a KFOR unit could expect to encounter. Thus, when some personnel, mostly from the 10th Mountain Division, began their MRE at Fort Polk, Louisiana, on 11 September, they thought it odd—if not extreme—to include in their exercise scenario terrorist attacks in New York, Pennsylvania, and Washington, D.C. The exercise participants soon realized that these terrorist attacks were real events, unrelated to the MRE for Kosovo. The MRE continued after only a brief pause: A peace enforcement mission in Kosovo required these units to deploy there by mid-October. Up to the eve of their departure, several of the deploying troops expected the mission to Kosovo to be scrubbed and to be sent farther east to Afghanistan. Other elements of the division would have their chance at that mission.

Although progress had been significant in pacifying the region and enforcing the peace in Kosovo, sufficient tension still caused periodic bursts of violence—albeit less frequently and less intensely than in years past. One such outburst occurred during the 2001–2002 Christmas–New Year holiday in the mixed Albanian and Serbian community of Kamenica, where Serbian children began fighting with Albanian children. This exchange rapidly escalated, with Albanians launching a public demonstration and throwing rocks at the U.S.-Russian KFOR personnel who arrived at the scene. An immediate curfew was imposed on the area, and the crowd dispersed; but the following week a Serb merchant was killed.

Both sides blamed the other for the violence and rising tension. Task Force FALCON responded to the situation with an intense campaign—meeting with community leaders, broadcasting frequent calls for calm over the radio, and distributing handbills to encourage the peaceful resolution of differences. The campaign worked. By the end of January, the tension in Kamenica had subsided, and even local Serbs acknowledged that the situation in their community was improving.

Farther south, in the town of Strpce, riots erupted after the newly elected mayor and his Albanian cabinet moved into the municipal building following the election described earlier. Protesting both their isolation and the authority of the Albanians, some Serbs blocked the main road leading into their part of the town. As the crowd grew unruly, some threw rocks at those officials who dared to appear in public. U.S. forces arrived in time to detain some of the more vocal Serbs, but not before the ethnic Albanians formed a crowd of their own, greater in number than the Serbs could muster. Responding to the situation, U.S. forces on-site arranged for the newly elected Albanian mayor to address the Albanian crowd and encourage people to disperse. Visibly shaken by their rowdy behavior, the leader nonetheless called for calm, even as he expressed subtle criticism of the nearby Serbs. Just as the Albanian crowd started to scatter, a UNMIK police car arrived on the scene, escorting a car with Serbian license plates. The Albanians became enraged, reassembled, and started throwing rocks at both vehicles. The few U.S. and Polish KFOR personnel at the scene quickly formed a thin circle around the vehicles. They were in danger of being overwhelmed by the surging crowd until a Ukrainian KFOR unit suddenly arrived to disperse the Albanians. The disturbance had all the makings of becoming a major incident with multiple casualties, but instead it was controlled and defused relatively quickly as a result of the disciplined and coordinated efforts of KFOR personnel. Impressed by the high caliber of Polish and Ukrainian soldiers at the scene, one Army battalion commander offered high praise, adding: "I'll take them to a riot any time."

The entire peace process in the province depended upon Serbs and Albanians working together to rebuild the severely damaged infrastructure. Without a united and cooperative civilian leadership, this process would be especially difficult. Generally, and at least within MNB-East, U.S. KFOR personnel found that the Albanian communities were unevenly split between a majority of moderates and a minority of extremists. Though receptive to ideas, the Albanian leaders often had a difficult time forging agreement among themselves. The fewer Serbian-dominant communities tended to be better organized and more competent, but they were uniformly critical of "outsiders." Although U.S. KFOR made every effort to protect Serbs from ethnic violence, Serbs rarely showed any appreciation.

It was a difficult dance to orchestrate—to get the two ethnic groups to move in concert. Many times, Task Force FALCON personnel either experienced frustration in getting Albanians and Serbs to work together, or else felt manipulated by both. For instance, after Serbian and Albanian representatives agreed to support digging a new well in a village outside Gnjilane, the Army arrived with the equipment to initiate the project only to discover that the proposed site was on private property. The Albanian municipal leadership refused to discuss restitution for the Serbian landowner, the two parties refused to cooperate with each other, and the Army refused to complete the project because property rights had been violated. Ultimately, the local government resolved to seize the property under eminent domain, which left the Army appearing complicit in delaying the project and then helping to seize the property on behalf of the Albanians.

Other problems resulted from the lingering legacy of the previous socialist regime. Years earlier, when Kosovo was an autonomous province in the Communist state of Yugoslavia, residential and commercial properties were not charged for electricity; but the policy collapsed along with Kosovo's infrastructure. Eventually, the provincial electric company was able to provide some semblance of consistent electrical service, and the utility company began to bill its customers. Years of socialism and free electricity were hard to overcome, however, and thousands of customers failed to pay their bills. Yet, as Army civil affairs personnel soon discovered, only Serbian communities had their electrical service terminated for failure to pay their invoices—and many families had never received a bill. Extensive negotiations involving U.S. KFOR personnel, Serbian community leaders, and the Albanian-managed electric company resulted in a restoration of electrical service in exchange for Serbian promises to pay invoices and permit meter readers on Serbian property.

An Elusive End State

In late 2002, when Operation JOINT GUARDIAN had been in place for three years, Task Force FALCON personnel began discussing "the end state": At what future or projected date would it be possible for U.S. KFOR personnel to significantly reduce their level of commitment and ultimately disengage? Episodes, like those cited above, made such a projection difficult. The fact that many other groups were involved in

Ethnic Albanians in Cernica stage a protest on 30 August 2000 after an Albanian man was arrested for allegedly killing two Serbian men and a four-year-old child.

the decision-making process made the difficulty only that much more so. Local Serbs had little affection for U.S. KFOR personnel in any case, protesting both their current presence and potential absence. Moderate Albanians were anxious over the possible departure of the Army, fearing a resurgence of Serbian violence or the return of Serbian security forces. Radical Albanians, on the other hand, were eager to see all KFOR units depart Kosovo. They hoped that their continuing acts of violence would hasten their ultimate objective of independence from Serbia, which only reinforced the necessity for Task Force FALCON to remain ever-vigilant—and present. Even some local UNMIK officials seemed ambivalent about the future of KFOR and slow to develop the civilian infrastructure that eventually would make the U.S. presence unnecessary.

In 2002, there was a clear resurgence of smuggling activities, but it also appeared that most of the contraband was being stopped at the border. Late in 2001, a new irritation had preceded this development when

Serbs begin to disburse in Domorovce after protesting the disappearance of two Serbs and accusing nearby Albanians of being responsible.

Serbia and Macedonia resolved their alleged border dispute, with Serbia voluntarily surrendering some land in Kosovo to the Macedonians. What might seem to have been a positive outcome resulted, unfortunately, in the loss by some ethnic Albanians of portions of their farmland. The land loss became yet another example for Kosovars to use to highlight their abuse by Serbia and to lend credibility to demands for independence. The result was to add more volatility to the region.

There was some tranquility to offset the tension. Markets and schools reopened, even if many were still ethnically segregated. Amid the shattered landscape also lay some areas virtually untouched. Days could pass in relative silence and routine, only to be suddenly disrupted by distant gunfire and a flurry of KFOR activity. Arriving in Kosovo, an Army chaplain lamented the tragedy that surrounded him and the necessity of viewing "the beauty of God's creation through a barbed wire fence."

The continuing mission to provide a safe and secure environment within MNB-East pulled Task Force FALCON in many directions. Radical Albanians continued to harass the Russians in and around Kamenica. In one ambush in early 2002, several Russians were killed and one U.S. soldier was wounded when their armored vehicles struck some land mines recently planted on a road. Infrequent mortar rounds or grenade attacks kept civilians on edge—and KFOR dashing across the countryside. At the same time, Task Force FALCON dealt with less dramatic episodes in the central zone, including multiple traffic violations, random gunfire, illegal weapon caches, and the discovery of a skeleton.

Serbs still experienced selective bullying, and they continued to yield to the pressure to leave Kosovo. Each month their population dwindled. Yet, the KFOR presence had made a difference. The number and frequency of Serbian departures was on the decline, as were the frequency and intensity of various violent acts—at least when compared with the recent past. Kosovo in mid-2002 was not what it had been in the early days of Operation JOINT GUARDIAN.

New success stories surfaced now as well. In Cernica—described by one staff officer as the "Tombstone" of Kosovo—Serb and Albanian leaders met to discuss community improvements and employment issues. The meeting required U.S. sponsorship (and U.S. mediation when the two parties slipped into old ethnic rivalries and disputes), but all the participants were encouraged that the meeting had occurred and that there was some resolution. In fact, during a recess and without any Americans present, the Serbian and Albanian leaders freely socialized. Violence still existed in Cernica, but, by the spring of 2002, Task Force FALCON characterized it as gang-related and criminal, unlike the ethnically oriented violence of three years earlier in which murder, arson, and grenade attacks were almost daily events.

That same spring, the commander of Task Force FALCON, Brig. Gen. Keith Huber, personally invited an equal number of Albanian and Serb high school students and their teachers from the Strpce area to visit Camp Bondsteel. An Army bus picked up the participants and escorted them to the Task Force FALCON main encampment for a full day that included tours of camp facilities, briefings, lunch, and a movie. Well received by all the participants, the explicit objective was to encourage the younger generation of both ethnic groups to become familiar with each other. "You don't want them to forget the pain," said the U.S. commander, "you just want them to realize that [the pain and hatred] can't be the future of Kosovo." Later that summer, a similar and larger initiative brought Albanian and Serb children together in a week-long summer camp. This effort, too, was credited as a significant success, along with several civic action projects in multiethnic communities in which Serbs and Albanians were required to work together.

By 2003, the level and intensity of violence in Kosovo had declined to such a point that the NATO forces throughout the province were able to reduce their total force structure. There had been a 20 percent drop in KFOR personnel in 2001 and another 20 percent drop in 2002. In MNB-East, a more mobile force of four thousand personnel provided a safe and secure environment in the U.S. area that once demanded more than seven thousand Americans plus another two thousand soldiers from Russia, Poland, Ukraine, and Greece. This drawdown of forces reduced or eliminated some security details. When a routine KFOR escort of Serbian shoppers traveling on public transportation was terminated in one municipality, no one noticed. In June 2003, the Russian peacekeepers were withdrawn from Kosovo. Another indication of the reduced threat level in 2003 was the elimination of Kevlar helmets and flak vests for routine patrols in selected areas of MNB-East.

The reduction of forces and the lowered level of violence in the province posed new operational challenges. To ensure that U.S. personnel did not lose their war-fighting skills, more time was devoted to training, which included creating and using firing ranges in Kosovo. In fact, gunfire heard in or near an American encampment after 2002 was more likely to be part of a military training exercise than hostile activities. During the latter half of 2002 and continuing into 2003, U.S. troops patrolled Kosovar neighborhoods with allied forces at least one week out of every month. Task Force FALCON characterized such joint patrols as constituting a multinational laboratory and a valuable learning experience for its personnel. Joint patrols also altered the operational tempo and helped prevent soldiers from becoming complacent in their peace-enforcement mission.

From a KFOR perspective, perhaps the most significant indication that conditions in Kosovo were beginning to change was that patrols were becoming routine, soldiers were more relaxed, and training was an integral component of each unit's weekly schedule. The two main encampments for Task Force FALCON—Camps Bondsteel and Monteith—looked like miniature replicas of long-established U.S. cantonments. Named after Medal of Honor recipients from the 1st Infantry Division, the facilities had rapidly grown at both sites from an odd assortment of tents in dirt fields to become small communities equipped with a surgical hospital, two gymnasiums, permanent barracks, paved roads, maintenance facilities, and a post exchange. The 750-acre complex of Camp Bondsteel, the headquarters for Task Force FALCON, had all the appearances of a typical Army installation. Although both camps were constructed quickly and designed to accommodate U.S. personnel to be stationed in Kosovo, a capital outlay in excess of $330 million suggested a long-term commitment, perhaps even a permanence, in the province. The U.S. presence also provided a welcomed boost to the local economy.

The Future of Kosovo

Ultimately, the situation in the province came to hinge on a question: What was the future of Kosovo to be? Was it to remain a province of Serbia and, if so, with what degree of autonomy, or was it to become an independent state? The potential for violence was always present, and the slightest provocation could easily erupt into a major conflagration. Even with the diminished level of violence, Army patrols consciously kept themselves visible—establishing a rapport with individuals in the community, nurturing friendly associations, and encouraging progress. U.S. KFOR personnel could not solve the multitude of problems that beleaguered the province, but they were able to facilitate the problem-solving process and provide some of the resources to start repairing the infrastructure. Within a six-month window (the standard tour of duty for the units that made up Task Force FALCON), leaders at all levels knew they could not end unemployment or raise levels of education. Neither could they stop smuggling completely or eliminate all organized crime. And there would always be individuals who nurtured ethnic hatred. Thus, the overriding objective remained to create a safe and secure environment within the province—one that would permit a civilian infrastructure to replace KFOR.

If the objective remained the same, the results continued to be uneven. In March 2004, violence flared up inexplicably. Ethnic Albanians burned Serb homes and churches, which prompted two days of rioting that resulted in the deaths of thirty-one people and the injury of hundreds of others. Task Force FALCON, recently reduced to two thousand personnel, needed and received a sudden reinforcement of five hundred soldiers. It was not long, however, before the force levels in MNB-East were reduced again, and no significant acts of violence occurred over the next two years.

Freedom of movement improved among all civilians residing in Kosovo as compared with years past. Ethnic Albanians and Serbians could travel on country roads and city streets in relative safety, without the fear of being shot at or attacked. Yet this freedom was tenuous and still not available among some segments of the population—particularly resident Serbs. The massive ethnic cleansing of neighborhoods was over, but random acts of ethnic violence still occurred, as did newer violence associated with organized crime and smuggling.

Early Morning Light *by Henrietta Snowden. This watercolor from the U.S. Army art collection depicts one of hundreds of Serbian Orthodox churches that were damaged during the ethnic conflict in Kosovo.*

By 2005, some Albanians and Serbs worked together in commercial enterprises and participated in educational institutions. Although hopeful signs, these examples were exceptions to the rule. Cordon and search operations still uncovered weapons caches, border patrols interdicted smugglers, and armed guards still protected certain Serbian facilities, such as the few remaining churches, which had been under constant guard since the early days of Operation JOINT GUARDIAN.

Task Force FALCON was officially created on 5 February 1999. In the seven years that followed, a wide assortment of Army organizations from both the active force and reserve components participated in the peace enforcement mission in Kosovo. Most of the units that made up Task Force FALCON served six-month tours and came from these divisions: 1st Infantry, 1st Armored, 101st Airborne, 82d Airborne, 10th Mountain, 3d Infantry, 28th Infantry (Pennsylvania National Guard), 38th Infantry (Indiana National Guard), 40th Infantry (California National Guard), 36th Infantry (Texas National Guard), and 29th Infantry (Virginia National Guard). The U.S. area for this peace enforcement mission in Kosovo originally was designated Multi-National Brigade (East), or simply abbreviated MNB-East. On 6 April 2006, reflecting its smaller force structure, the U.S. area was redesignated as Multi-National Task Force (East). As of 2007, it was still unclear when the continued presence of Task Force FALCON would cease to be a necessity in Kosovo.

Summary and Analysis

Operation JOINT GUARDIAN posed unique challenges for American military personnel in Kosovo, because it required them to develop new ways of thinking—particularly about peace enforcement and peacekeeping operations. Restraint and patience in the face of hostility, and calm in response to anger, were concepts that had carried little weight during their basic training. Now they mattered. Although their traditional combat training had taught them to prize concealment, their mission to enforce peace caused them to put appearances first. Rather than holding their firearms in a readiness mode, soldiers carried their weapons pointed toward the ground. The troops adapted to these requirements quickly, reflecting both their high caliber of training and individual responsibility. Their focused and mission-oriented sense of duty amazed commanders and outside observers.

The awkward deployment of Task Force HAWK and problems with the initial U.S. insertion into Kosovo troubled military commanders. Both tasks were completed, but because contingency plans for rapid deployment were inflexible, yet not always defined in full, nothing went as smoothly as expected. Line units assigned to specific sectors, for example, were not always aware of the activities of civil affairs units, which operated over larger areas.

The lack of information-sharing left a wide gap in which organizations could and did work at cross-purposes. A local commander might resolve a dispute between an Albanian and a Serb in favor of the Serb, only to learn some time later that the Albanian had appealed to a passing Military Police vehicle, whose occupants, in all innocence, had reversed the decision. Complicating matters, training and doctrine among the various NATO forces were not always consistent. Some of those units were unprepared to deal with riots. Others had specific instructions to refrain from guarding certain sites, even though they might be subject to arson or vandalism.

After U.S. forces settled into a "battle rhythm," leaders at all levels became well aware of their ability to dominate every problem and solution. Having the organizational structure, training, and resources necessary to handle all kinds of issues, the officers of Task Force FALCON tended, at first, to take the lead in resolving matters without including other parties to the process. As it became clear, however, that such assertiveness contributed little to solving Kosovo's long-term problems, the commanders of U.S. forces eventually refrained from dominating situations in order to encourage Albanians, Serbs, UNMIK, and the NGOs present in the province to take the initiative themselves.

One of the great advantages that the Kosovo mission possessed was the opportunity it gave many soldiers to learn how to operate in a demanding peace-enforcement environment. The American force had come to Kosovo to stop the horrible violence afflicting the province's Albanians. In short order, however, those victims became the victimizers. Most of the resources of Task Force FALCON were used to protect Serbs. The bloodshed had no sooner ended, moreover, than U.S. forces found themselves dealing with smugglers, revenge seekers, and radical revolutionaries bent on achieving independence for Kosovo at whatever cost.

As they prepared for the mission, some within the American military had looked for instruction to the most recent U.S. experience in the region, the effort in Bosnia-Herzegovina. The parallels they found, however, were few. Although Kosovo and Bosnia had both been part of Yugoslavia and the conflict in each involved clashes between ethnic Serbians and either Albanians or Bosnians, the differences were significant. First and foremost, Bosnia had been an independent country, whereas Kosovo was a province of Serbia. In Bosnia, a relative demographic balance existed among its several ethnic populations, including Croatians, Serbians, and Bosnian-Muslims (or Bosniacs). In Kosovo in 2005, by contrast, almost nine out of ten people were ethnic Albanians, and most of the rest were Serbs. Although the civil war in Bosnia had severely damaged that nation's infrastructure, parts of the country were able to continue functioning. The conflict in Kosovo, however, had resulted in the virtual demolition of all public services and utilities. Finally, Bosnia had the buffer of a no-man's-zone to separate its feuding groups, but Kosovo did not. As a result, the members of the various factions in Bosnia enjoyed freedom of movement as long as they refrained from attempting to cross the line into another group's territory. In Kosovo, however, Serbs were intermingled among Albanians at random. Even when the Serbs withdrew into enclaves, the areas they occupied were so small and isolated that they had little freedom of movement.

Compared with Bosnia, conditions in Kosovo also posed new operational challenges to the American military, some of them daunting. In Bosnia, for example, Task Force EAGLE worked mainly out of its principal base camps. Because of the nature of the violence in Kosovo, however, U.S. personnel had to move continually from place to place to remain on top of their assignments, so platoon- and squad-size command posts and checkpoints were much more the rule. This situation imposed significant logistical and operational demands that diminished only gradually, as the level of violence declined.

One of the unfortunate legacies of the war in Bosnia was the overwhelming number of land mines and explosives scattered across the country. Still, nearly all of the minefields ultimately were identified and isolated or neutralized. Kosovo, on the other hand, experienced nearly the opposite situation, one that was even less fortunate. Although not nearly as much live ordnance was used in Kosovo as in Bosnia, it was placed more randomly and thus was that much harder to find. The mines and booby traps that the various antagonists had hidden tended to come to light only when they exploded.

Even so, there was no denying that Operation JOINT GUARDIAN achieved major, measurable successes. Although some eight hundred thousand ethnic Albanians had fled Kosovo in the 1990s, for example, almost as many returned after NATO forces entered the province to enforce peace. Such a massive return of people to their homes was perhaps the most satisfying measure of operational success and a direct reflection of the situation on the ground: The level of violence had diminished, a measure of law and order had been reestablished, schools and stores were reopened, free elections became possible, public services came back on line, and most of Kosovo's civilians once more had freedom of movement. Overall, the consensus among many Kosovars—both Albanian and Serbian—was that living conditions had indeed improved.

The question nonetheless persisted: What would the political future of the province be? Although it had little bearing on the day-to-day work of the forces guarding Kosovo, the answer would determine when they would go home. For many officers, eliminating chronic unemployment, invigorating an anemic economy, and rebuilding the infrastructure of the province held the most promise for achieving security. But the absence of a political end state discouraged long-term solutions and hampered the ability of the American military to do anything more than react to each exigency that arose.

Whether such a reactive posture would be enough, however, to sustain the province as it moved toward political revitalization, no one could tell, for many obstacles remained, including the fragile state of Serbia, to which Kosovo remained attached as a subordinate subdivision. The economy in Serbia was a shambles. One-third of that nation's population was living below the poverty line. Of its 670,000 refugees in 2000, 30 percent had fled from Kosovo. Meanwhile, if violence against Kosovo's Muslims had all but ceased, hard feelings remained. Serbs, in particular, insisted almost universally that, whatever the excesses of their own group in Kosovo during the 1990s, Albanian atrocities exceeded anything they had done.

More important, the Serbs were certain that the presence of the UN protectorate in Kosovo was temporary. They looked forward to their return to power in a Serb-controlled province after NATO left. Most of Kosovo's Albanians, for their part, wanted nothing of the sort, and a small minority persisted in its pursuit of independence. U.S. forces, as a result, had little choice but to continue their efforts to find and to seize weapons caches, to disrupt the flow of smuggled ordnance across porous borders, and to remain on the alert to stifle rabble-rousers and other provocateurs.

It would be too much to say, however, that the future of the province was not without promise. On 21 November 2005, representatives from Kosovo and Serbia met under UN sponsorship in Kosovo's capital, Pristina, to discuss the future of the region. The Albanian majority insisted on Kosovo's complete independence, whereas the Serbs offered the province considerable autonomy. In spite of the wide gulf between the two positions, both sides were at least talking to each other and willing to continue the negotiations, which certainly would have been unthinkable six years earlier.

The road that led to this small milestone in Operation JOINT GUARDIAN and in Kosovo's history was long and tedious. Yet even after the operation had been in place only one year, already military observers could see progress that might eventually lead to a lasting peace in the province. In 2000, Task Force FALCON's commander, Brig. Gen. Keith Huber, assessed the situation in Kosovo this way:

> So are we safe and secure? For the moment. Is it tense? Yes. Are these people capable of momentary violence? Yes. Is there hatred here? Yes. But it's like any other society in the world. And at least the people of Kosovo are moving forward on a democratic path, and at least they are trying, some of them willingly, some of them grudgingly. But they are being assisted along this path of democracy, which says that you accept diversity, you tolerate

> differences, and you try to provide a better life for your children than you had.

Later in 2000, Albanian and Serb high school students who had visited Camp Bondsteel together for a full day of briefings and activities sent notes of appreciation to Huber. All of the notes were translated and saved as evidence that the eventual resolution of the crisis in Kosovo might indeed bring peace to the troubled land. One Albanian girl wrote: "My wish for the future of Kosova was and will remain that our place has a better future. . . . I want the hate and violence to not exist any place in the world." And an ethnic Serbian boy wrote: "I can see a great future in Kosovo without. . . . violence and hate and killing."

Peace and a better future for Kosovo seemed like fanciful illusions as Task Force FALCON entered that troubled land in June 1999. Given the level of violence and destruction, and the intense hatred among the ethnic groups, no one could have foreseen that serious negotiations between Serbians and Albanians would be possible only six years later. The events of Operation JOINT GUARDIAN were extraordinarily frustrating and difficult but, as Lt. Col. Timothy Reese, commander of Task Force 1-77th Armor, wrote after boarding his plane for home late in 1999, there were compensations and hope:

> We gave everything we had to fulfilling our tasks and could remember hundreds of small successes. We saved many lives, prevented the killing of many others, delivered life saving aid to tens of thousands of people, and did our best to get Serbs and Albanians, Catholics and Gypsies to work together for a brighter future in Kosovo. And for the first time in the lives of Kosovars, they experienced a conquering Army that did not loot, and rape and kill. It did not seem arrogant for me to think about the line in the biblical Beatitudes: "Blessed are the peacemakers."

Further Readings

Although there are many references to the conflict in Kosovo, the majority of the publicly accessible publications generally fall between those that end before NATO involvement in 1999 and those that focus on a very small aspect of the conflict. Readers searching for a broad overview of military operations surrounding the war in Kosovo should visit the NATO web site at http://www.nato.int/kosovo/history.htm. Small archival collections of oral history interviews, unit histories, after-action reports, and various documents and unpublished manuscripts are in the custody of the U.S. Army Center of Military History at Fort McNair in Washington, D.C., and the U.S. Army Heritage and Education Center at Carlisle Barracks, Pennsylvania. Among the dozens of published works, readers may want to consider the following references:

Buckley, William Joseph, ed. *Kosovo: Contending Voices on Balkan Interventions*. Grand Rapids, Mich.: William B. Eerdmans Publishing Co., 2000.

Cordesman, Anthony H. *The Lessons and Non-Lessons of the Air and Missile Campaign in Kosovo*. Westport, Conn.: Praeger Publishers, 2001.

Daalder, Ivo H., and Michael E. O'Hanlon. *Winning Ugly: NATO's War To Save Kosovo*. Washington, D.C.: Brookings Institution Press, 2000.

Judah, Tim. *Kosovo: War and Revenge*. New Haven, Conn.: Yale University Press, 2000.

Kirkpatrick, Charles E. *"Ruck It Up!" The Post–Cold War Transformation of V Corps, 1990–2001*. Washington, D.C.: U.S. Army Center of Military History, 2006.

Malcolm, Noel. *Kosovo: A Short History*. New York: HarperCollins Publishers, 1999.

Nardulli, Bruce R., Walter L. Perry, Bruce Pirnie, John Gordon, and John G. McGinn. *Disjointed War: Military Operations in Kosovo, 1999*. Santa Monica, Calif.: Rand Corporation, 2002.

Nation, R. Craig. *War in the Balkans, 1992–2002*. Carlisle Barracks, Pa.: Strategic Studies Institute, 2003.

Cover: Checkpoint 65, located on the Kosovo side of the Ground Safety Zone separating Kosovo from the Federal Republic of Yugoslavia.
All photos from Department of Defense.

CMH Pub 70–109–1

www.ingramcontent.com/pod-product-compliance
Lightning Source LLC
LaVergne TN
LVHW050543100826
845148LV00002B/659

* 9 7 8 1 7 8 2 6 6 2 8 7 7 *